Already a
Writer at
Six or Sixteen

Theresa M. Sull

authorHOUSE

AuthorHouse™
1663 Liberty Drive
Bloomington, IN 47403
www.authorhouse.com
Phone: 1 (800) 839-8640

Published by AuthorHouse   03/20/2020

ISBN: 978-1-4685-4852-5 (sc)
ISBN: 978-1-4685-4853-2 (e)

Library of Congress Control Number: 2012901836

Print information available on the last page.

Any people depicted in stock imagery provided by Thinkstock are models, and such images are being used for illustrative purposes only.
Certain stock imagery © Thinkstock.

This book is printed on acid-free paper.

Contents

Billboards

Appendices

Dedication

This work is dedicated to my loving husband Gene,
and to my talented daughters Linnet and Julia.

Acknowledgements

I acknowledge, with deep gratitude, all the students I met in 30 years of teaching. My students taught me much more than I ever taught them.

Introduction

YOU PROBABLY TWISTED A FEW paper chains when you were young, but right now try to think of paper chains as much more than a child's handicraft. Think of paper chains as a metaphor for literacy.

Devising paper chains requires a small amount of precision, but each chain can be improved through individual creativity. The design of a paper chain calls for skills of sequencing and patterning, but the color, edges, size, and texture of the paper can vary. The basics are simple, but innovations are infinite!

Paper chains, like children's language and literacy development, are flexible but fragile. Today you can buy pre-cut strips of colored paper with prepared sticky ends to be twisted into links, but when I was a child we cut our own strips of construction paper, and used homemade flour and water paste to form the links. We hung paper chains from the dining room chandelier as a party decoration, and we wore paper chains as crowns when we pretended to be royalty.

History demonstrates that paper and pen have been the most significant medium of human communication. Although writing on clay or stone tablets predates paper, and oral communication predates any writing, writing preserved on paper has most effectively carried human language across physical space and time.

Even now, when we can send writing electronically by fax or e-mail, many of us carefully save a paper copy. When we read a book we're sometimes hearing voices from the past, even from the distant past, because good books have long-lasting strength, like steel implements forged over flame. Because literacy supports human connections across space and time like the links of a chain support a bridge, we can send messages to the future by writing down our poems, plays, songs, stories, and essays.

Those children who are well supported by paper chains as they learn to read and write will follow a typical path as they develop their literacy skills. Supportive adults can use my informative BILLBOARDS along the road to literacy, and they will applaud as their children achieve notable MILESTONES along the route.

The fragility of paper chains reminds us that in spite of the critical importance of literacy in our world, not all our children will become strong readers and writers. Unfortunately, paper chains are easily torn and broken! But just as anyone can design a paper chain, anyone can learn to support literacy, creating a valuable link in a lengthy chain.

CHAPTER 1

Already a Writer at Six

THE WORD *WRITE* IS DEFINED in more than fifteen ways, and these don't include related expressions like *write down, write in, write off,* or *write up.* W*riter,* however, is defined simply as *one who writes,* especially as a profession. *Author* is a synonym for *writer,* traced to the Latin word for *creator,* a definition that hints at the power of writing!

To write is to create. A writer can create new personalities, intriguing relationships, or entirely new worlds. When we teach a six-year-old to write, we are offering a gift of creative self-empowerment. But what's the best way to teach children to write? Are some teaching methods more effective than others? Can some methods actually inhibit a child's progress? What if your child is not interested in writing? Some parents and other teachers wonder if their children's writing skills are developing well enough, or fast enough. They can find reassuring answers in *Already A Writer At Six or Sixteen.*

MILESTONES ALONG A WRITER'S PATH

Child's Age	Developmental Skills Attained
12 months	Picks up cereal or raisins with a pincer grasp
	Holds crayon in fist to make marks on paper
	Say three words beyond *mama* and *dada*
18 months	Scribbles with a marker or crayon
	Points to simple pictures like *dog* or *cat*
	Begins pretend play

1

2 years	Scribbles, usually staying on the paper
	Says 2-word phrases
	Names pictures like *plane*, *apple*, *man*
	Answers questions about simple choices

2 ½ years	Throws toys, then tracks them visually
	Holds crayons in fingers, not fist
	Uses 2-3 word sentences
	Refers to self and others with pronouns
	Uses *ing* endings, simple past tense verbs

3 years	Makes *pancakes*, *snakes*, or *balls* of dough
	Imitates drawing a *circle* and a *cross*
	Gives names to paintings and drawings
	Uses 3-4 word sentences
	Asks simple questions

| 3 ½ years | Describes a simple sequence of events |
| | Demonstrates peer imitation by parallel play |

4 years	Traces vertical lines, then horizontal lines
	Draws a person with 2 body parts
	Drawings and paintings are recognizable
	Understands *in front, behind, above, below*

5 years	Sews on a simple sewing card
	Makes recognizable objects of dough or clay
	Holds a pencil correctly when shown
	Traces letters and simple shapes
	Draws a person with 3 to 4 body parts
	Uses sentences averaging 5 words

6 years	Vocabulary of 10,000 words
	Draws a person with 5 to 7 body parts
	Copies his/her first and last name

| | Speaks sentences averaging 6 words |
| | Reads common signs like *stop* and *exit* |

7 years	Draws a person with 8 to 10 body parts
	Prints dictated upper and lower case letters
	Speaks in sentences averaging 7 words
	Reads color and number words
	Grasps simple double meanings in jokes

12 years	Vocabulary approaching 30,000 words
	Argues and debates with familiar people
	Improving ability to plan and self-regulate
	Begins to understand sarcasm and irony
	Writes poems, paragraphs, complete stories
	Creates an organized character sketch

13 to 16 years	Vocabulary up to 40,000 words
	Chooses friends based on common interests
	Gaining physical, sexual maturation
	Demonstrates more emotional control
	Classifies others as smart, sporty, nerdy, etc.
	Considers dating, especially in groups
	Conscious choice of style and fashion
	Wants to fit in with a group of teenagers
	Values athletic and/or artistic achievements
	Uses research references effectively
	Can use accepted syntax, vocabulary, style
	Uses similes and metaphors to express ideas

Although no child moves along the developmental path in exactly the same way as any other child, these typical milestones provide a general guide to children's progress. You can learn more about children's milestones of development from a trained teacher, a pediatrician, or a child psychologist. Psychologists use assessment instruments like the *Brigance Diagnostic Inventory of Early Development*, the *Kaufman Survey of Early Academic and Language Skills*, the *McCarthy Scales of Children's Abilities*, the *Stanford-Binet IQ Test*, the *Wide Range Assessment of Visual Motor Ability*, and other exams.

American children often start first grade as six-year-olds. Theorists of development have a lot to say about this age group, so I've summarized their ideas in *Appendix I: Influential Theorists of Development and Early Education.* For example, the psychosocial theory of Erik Erikson states that in children from the ages of three to six, *initiative* is often pitted against undesirable feelings of *guilt*. Children whose parents and other teachers expect too much self-discipline can encourage too much guilt, leading to low risk-taking in their children. Isn't it better to appreciate the natural initiative of young children, which is necessary for the creativity that writers need?

Six-year-olds still use pretend play to explore future roles. That's why children ambitiously and frequently try out new behaviors on their own initiative, but this tendency can annoy the adults around them! For example, one boy I taught when I was a student teacher in a public kindergarten pulled down his pants at *Circle Time*. While the whole class watched, Kenneth urinated on the carpet.

My supervising teacher was an exceptionally wise woman. Ruth didn't look appalled or surprised, but simply asked the boy to get paper towels from the restroom so they could clean up the floor together. I think Kenneth was actually demonstrating his masculinity by marking his territory in a creative way. Wasn't he asserting himself as mammals have done for thousands of years? Of course, eventually Kenneth would find a better way to express himself, through his writing instead of a shocking action.

The kindergarten year is the time for parents to start leaving simple notes on mirrors and in lunch boxes, and it's a time to offer interesting art materials to children. These include paper of different textures, paste or glue, non-toxic paints, colorful markers, and dough and clay. To promote their children's healthy development, parents and other teachers will gather equipment and materials like those listed in *Billboard B.*

Researchers have proposed that children's first six years are a time of galloping development in all domains. A time when parents and other teachers need to carefully examine young children's environments and activities, ensuring that they promote adequate language development. To help you assess your child's world, the critical *Components of a Language-Rich Environment* are listed below.

COMPONENTS OF A LANGUAGE-RICH ENVIRONMENT

LISTENING AND TALKING

- Cradle children with language all day long: Speak warmly and make eye contact.
- Play rhyming games, word games, lotto and board games with children.
- Talk about visual displays like magazine pictures and photos of children.
- Label objects and areas, occasionally moving and changing the signs.
- Describe and explain your actions all day: ("I'm going to mix up some paint now.")
- Talk about what will happen soon in school and at the playground.
- Use puppets and stuffed animals to 'talk' to children.
- Use tape recorders so children can hear themselves talk.
- Use books on tape that children can follow in print.
- Initiate conversations with children about families, their meals and other activities.
- Be an active and reflective listener for your children.
- Compliment children with specifics: ("Great! You put on your shirt by yourself.")
- Encourage children to talk to people: ("Tell Mrs. S about . . . Ask Jamal about . . .")
- Encourage children to use words, not actions, to show feelings or to solve problems.
- Take dictation to record a child's ideas and stories: Read them aloud to a child.
- Have conversations with other adults to provide good language models.

MUSIC AND MOVEMENT

Sing and play recordings of traditional songs:

- Folk songs (*This train is bound for glory, this train*)
- Camp songs (*There were ten in a bed and the little one said, Roll over, roll over*)
- Holiday songs (*Jingle Bells; Here comes Peter Cottontail; Chanukah, O Chanukah*)
- Action and Circle Game songs (*If you're happy and you know it, Clap your hands*)
- Finger Play Songs (*Here Are Grandma's Spectacles; The Itsy Bitsy Spider*)
- Songs about daily events (*Circle Time, Take a little nap, Close your tired eyes*)
- Ask children to make up their own songs about their activities.
- Have children dance while acting out the words of songs.
- Have children draw or paint pictures to illustrate songs, poems, and stories.

POETRY

- Chant finger plays with children (*Here is the church, Here is the steeple*)
- Recite short children's poems (*One Misty, Moisty Morning; Mix a Pancake*)
- Read aloud children's poetry by compelling and/or amusing poets (*Margaret Wise Brown, Mary Ann Hoberman, Langston Hughes, Bill Martin, Jr., Shel Silverstein*)
- Help children create their own poems and silly sayings.

Parents and other teachers can make learning fun for children with language play, including *rhyming, chanting, call-and-response, name games,* and *silly sounds.* A game of *Bingo* can be good early practice for letter recognition. Beginners' card games like *Lotto* will improve concentration and memory, important skills for reading and writing. In *The Name Game,* children substitute beginning sounds to make rhyming words, a skill necessary for learning phonics. Whether chanted or sung to a simple melody, *The Name Game* is an enjoyable and educational pre-reading activity. I'm old enough to remember this tune as a novelty hit recorded by Shirley Ellis in 1965!

THE NAME GAME

Jane, Jane, bow-bane,*
Banana fanna, fow-fane,
Fee, fie, mow-mane . . . Jane!

(**Mike, Mike, bow-bike . . . or Linda Binda bow-binda . . .*)

Generations of teachers, camp counselors, and parents organizing children's birthday parties have directed *circle games*, which are organized activities for groups of children. In addition to being a good management tool, old-fashioned circle games can facilitate the development of skills needed for literacy. In many educational settings, *Circle Time* (or *Meeting* or *Group Time*) offers an opportunity for adults to support children's development in all these areas: sensory, gross motor, fine motor, cognitive, language, social, and emotional skills.

Can you sing and dance the *Hokey Pokey*? Do you know the *Chicken Dance*, the *Bunny Hop*, or the *Macarena*? Traditional games and simple line dances promote strength in a child's trunk and arms. Circle games also aide developing balance, bilateral coordination, dominance, auditory skills, and the development of concepts like prepositions. When you make up rhyming lyrics for wordless dances, you're supporting language development as your children are practicing their physical skills.

THE HOKEY POKEY

You put your right hand* in,
You take your right hand out,
You put your right hand in,
And you shake it all about!
You do the Hokey Pokey,
And you turn yourself around,
That's what it's all about!

(*Insert left hand, right leg, belly, bottom . . .)

Over time, human beings develop in at least seven distinct areas, described below. Because wise parents and other teachers respect the interconnected nature of child development, they provide activities and materials that support all the areas of development in children, which go well beyond memorization and rote recitation.

AREAS OF HUMAN DEVELOPMENT

Sensory Perception gives meaning to information taken in by the senses through seeing, hearing, touching, smelling, tasting, and less obvious senses like proprioception. Later, the children will express such sensory experiences in their speech and in their writing, increasing interest and complexity.

Gross Motor Skills use the large muscles of the body for trunk, leg, and arm strength; balance; bilateral coordination; dominance of hand and foot; ability to cross the midline; and agility. Gross motor skills help children move about with ease to gain all types of information. Large muscle development also allows children to sit still for long periods for reading, writing, or typing.

Fine Motor Skills use small muscles of the mouth, eyes, and fingers. Chewing, swallowing, talking, singing, and *signing* use fine motor skills. Fine motor strength, dexterity, and coordination will help children with manuscript writing and keyboarding.

Language Skills include listening, speaking, singing, *signing*, articulation, intonation, rhyming, vocabulary building, rhythm for fluency, and concept development. Writing can be considered a language skill that depends on all these other skills of communication.

Cognitive or Intellectual Skills like thinking and reasoning involve memory, problem solving, learning through imitation, following directions, creativity, patterning, sequencing, and symbolic representation. Cognitive skills are used in math and logic, as well as for speaking, reading and writing.

Social Skills involve respecting other people, turn-taking, sharing space, enjoying peer interaction, learning courtesy, co-operating in groups, and group identity. Later these social skills will be necessary for all higher education, and for employment. To become leaders, politicians usually excel in social skills, and those who don't are often derided by their colleagues and the general public.

Emotional Skills include experiencing joy, recognizing and expressing emotions, empathizing with the emotions of others, and tolerating frustration. Emotional skills are very important tools for a satisfying adult life.

Circle games may seem old-fashioned, but they can enhance every area of children's development. Teachers of young children can observe in several classrooms to learn unfamiliar songs, finger plays, and games. A book from a public library or bookstore can add more circle time activities to a teacher's repertoire. Props like scarves, rhythm sticks, hats, shakers and bells add excitement to group activities.

By choosing cards with illustrated titles of songs and games, children can take turns choosing their group's next activity. Remember that children sometimes like to be in charge. They tend to choose their favorite songs over and over, so seasonally rotate your cards to keep interest high.

Many different ethnic groups have traditional games that can enrich understanding of their own and other people's heritage. Stretch yourself! Learn something new from a less familiar culture and then teach it to your children. Before you try a new activity, however, think about what this specific game or song involves. Is it too easy or too hard for the children in your group? What skills can be practiced in this activity? Make *Circle Time* educational as well as fun by covering important concepts everyday *(Billboard A)*.

BILLBOARD A: Circle Time Concepts to Cover

Animals: Insects, Pets, Birds
Feelings All People Have
Geology: Gravel, Rocks, Soil
People: Ages, Height, Weight
Plants: Flowers, Grass, Trees
Shapes: In Everyday Objects
Time, Clocks, Calendar
Transportation: Types of
Weather: Storms, Deserts

What kinds of circle activities should you try? You're limited only by your imagination! Circle games can involve singing, dancing, movement, imitation, improvisation, call and response, and more. The games can be very simple or quite complex. Work up to complicated circle games slowly, so children can experience success as they skip along the developmental path, really enjoying these small-group activities.

Gathering a group of children is made easier with the use of a routine. Use a signal like the tinkle of a hand bell, or sing a special song. Soon your children will begin to join the group out of habit, because they've enjoyed *Circle Time* so many times in the past. Sound a warning about five minutes before you begin circle games, to let the children bring closure to their ongoing activities, which demonstrates your respect for a child's interests.

CIRCLE RIGHT NOW*

Meeting, meeting, meeting,
Let's go to the meeting,
Circle, circle, circle . . . Right now!
Welcome to our meeting,
We need you at our meeting,
Circle, circle, circle . . . Right now!

(*Can be sung to the tune of TV's *Rawhide!*)

STEP RIGHT UP

It's circle time,
Step right up, sit right down!
It's talking time,
Step right up, sit right down!
It's listening time,
Step right up, sit right down!
It's meeting time, right now.

PUTTING THINGS AWAY

We're putting the blocks* away,
We hope it won't take all day,
We've got to get done
If we want to have fun,
We're putting the blocks away!

(*Insert toys, dolls, clay, books, etc.)

I LIKE THE WAY

I like the way that Ellen is cleaning,
I like the way that Ethan is cleaning,
I like the way that Tanya is cleaning,
I think we're ready for Circle Time!

School children's circle songs can be traced at least to the late 19th century. Patty Smith Hill, an innovator in the movement for progressive education in the United States, wrote the now famous song, *Happy Birthday to You!* To the same melody she sang *Good Morning to You!* recognizing each child in her group individually. Gathering and greeting songs have been preserved as part of human history, but parents and other teachers can compose their own melodies to my songs of invitation, above.

Most children love to hear their names sung by the group, but what if children are reluctant to join a large group for circle activities? Never force a child to join your circle! Instead, for the children who don't feel ready to play with the large group yet, provide quiet activities like looking at books or completing puzzles. Set up a plan with other adults who can help uninvolved children choose quiet activities during circle time. They should help disruptive children become constructively involved.

How can you begin to make the most of *Circle Time*? First, jot down the circle games you know. I bet you've played *Simon Says* or sang *Head, Shoulders, Knees and Toes*. The folk game *'A' My Name Is Alice* provides practice with beginning consonant and vowel sounds. *('B' my name is Bobby, and I come from Boston, and I'm bringing baked beans.)* In the party game *Telephone*, children whisper to each other trying to repeat the phrase traveling around the circle. With hilarious and sometimes intentional mistakes, the children are practicing their skills of auditory discrimination, which will be necessary for encoding when children begin to write.

Games for groups and games for individual children have a place in preschool and kindergarten classrooms, because most young children love to be playful or silly!

When we introduce alphabet games like *The Name Game,* we increase children's knowledge of the encoding and decoding processes. This early exposure to phonics can help children learn to read and write the meaningful sounds of their language.

Young children often enjoy pre-reading 'workbooks' of simple puzzles that require letter matching by sight. As five- and six-year-olds begin to understand *letter-sound correspondence*, they can enjoy drawing lines between pictures of objects and letters that represent beginning sounds. Some children enjoy tracing geometric shapes and letters, or other pre-writing activities. McGraw-Hill publishes a variety of workbooks for different ages on subjects like phonics and beginning math. You can find these workbooks in a large bookstore, or on-line at www.mhlearningstore.com.

Computer games can help children practice reading and writing skills like eye-hand coordination, letter recognition, letter-sound correspondence, sight word recognition and beginning phonics. But be careful when ordering computer games because some software uses only flashy cartoons to hold children's attention. Look for computer games that encourage creativity. In fact, be very cautious about any use of workbooks and computer software! These commercial products might make reading and writing seem boring, or even excessively complicated. Many so-called educational aides are not actually teaching but only drilling, or testing what children have already learned.

Still, success with drills and puzzles is not necessarily a bad thing. Such accomplishments can be affirming, especially when reading skills are new. Remember, however, that most children will learn to read and write in any language-rich environment, without any commercial products. What children really need are adults who respond to children's natural interest in literacy!

Think about this for a moment. Did Bill Gates or Steve Jobs (or William Shakespeare, Emily Dickinson, Agatha Christie, or Langston Hughes) have personal computers when they were little? Of course not, but they did have many experiences that facilitated their language and motor development. Experiences like listening to books read aloud, building models, and playing circle games. Experiences that prepared them to invent personal computers and software, or to write great poems, plays, stories, and novels.

To encourage children's writing, wise grown-ups facilitate children's development by providing appropriate fine motor equipment and materials, such as those listed in *Billboard B*. Healthy fine motor development is a wonderful basis for writing skills, but remember that *language development* is much more important! You can combine language and fine motor development by talking with children about their physical activities, or by taking dictation about children's arts-and-crafts projects.

BILLBOARD B: Fine Motor Equipment and Materials

Building toys
Cardboard shapes to trace
Chalk and crayons
Checkers and chess pieces
Clay and play dough
Dolls and doll clothes
Jigsaw puzzles
Markers and colored pencils
Paints and paint brushes
Paste and non-toxic glue
Plastic dishes and play food

Ribbon, string, and yarn
Sand and dry rice
Small cars and trucks
Small, safe staplers

Almost all children can use their small muscles to be creative. Children with a physical disability like cerebral palsy, which could interfere with fine motor development, still can become skillful writers. Parents and other teachers will rely on children's cognitive skills to supplement their fine motor skills as they limber up the little fingers of future writers.

Young children usually love *water play,* whether in a sink, in a bathtub, at the beach, at a swimming pool, in a plastic dishpan, or in a commercial water table. Water play involves actions like pouring and splashing. Children can even *'paint'* with water, using clean brushes of different sizes to make disappearing marks on sidewalks or buildings.

Water play tools that can be found around the house include plastic cups, funnels, and turkey basters *(Billboard C)*. Small toys, such as a doll that needs a bath, doll clothes, plastic dishes, toy boats and cars, or wind-up fish and turtles, can be stored in a convenient bin. In addition to exercising fine motor skills, water play can teach basic science concepts like *absorb, dissolve, empty, evaporate, full, pour, strain,* and *stir*.

Sophisticated language learning can take place only if wise adults talk to children about what's going on as they play in the water. Experiments to find out what sinks or floats is a typical preschool or kindergarten experience involving concepts of physics. Water play will be cooling in the summer, and is always soothing to the spirit. A warm bath can offer an hour of educational water play for children at home if you provide the right toys and careful supervision. Never leave children unattended in bathtubs, wading pools or with buckets of water! Drowning is both quick and tragic.

BILLBOARD C: Water Play Tools

Clothes Sprinklers
Colanders
Funnels
Measuring Cups
Mixing Bowls

Pitchers

Racks for Drying

Shampoo Bottles

Slotted Spoons

Soap Dispensers

Socks

Sponges

Squeeze Bottles

Towels

Turkey Basters

Wash Cloths

Dough and/or clay are standard materials to support the concept of representation, as well as children's fine motor development. Children can squeeze and stretch dough or clay, providing exercise opportunities to strengthen fingers and hands for writing. *Play-Doh©*, *Silly Putty©*, *Sculpty©* or modeling clays can be purchased in craft or toy stores, or mix up a batch of play dough at home from a recipe below. Playing with dough or clay invites children's healthy actions, such as those in *Billboard D*.

Making snakes, ropes, pancakes, pie crusts, or snowballs of dough uses both hands in bilateral integration, and encourages weight-bearing of the arms. Standing at a low table or kneeling at a coffee table promotes weight-bearing in the legs. A commercial *Play-Doh Factory©* is intriguing, but there are many tools for dough already in your house. The tools you select could include cookie cutters, dull knives, forks, a garlic press, scissors, spoons, old prickly plastic hair rollers, and plastic or wooden spools from thread.

BILLBOARD D: Clay and Play Dough Actions

Flatten

Fold

Imprint

Mold

Pat

Poke

Pound

Roll Out

Sculpt

Slap

Slice

Squeeze

Stretch

Weigh

Grains of sand, or dry rice and beans, are tiny solids that act like liquids when placed in a wide container or a sand box. They can be poured and measured or, transferred from hand to hand, will run right through little fingers like water! Much of the same equipment you provide for water play also works for sand play, such as bowls, measuring cups, spoons, and tiny toys that can be buried.

A sandbox set up outdoors should be covered to prevent neighborhood cats from using it. Sand can scratch toys like painted metal trucks or plastic bowls, so monitor the tools and equipment used with sand. Prompt disposal of damaged toys demonstrates to children a respect for their belongings.

Typical early science learning includes experimenting to learn about ways that dried rice and beans or sand *do not* act like water. Will anything sink in a bowl of dry rice? Remember that bins of dry beans, rice, water, and sand must be monitored. Undesirable mold, algae or insects could grow in them, but they will last for years if kept away from moisture. Water tables and plastic bins must be emptied and refilled regularly, and cleaned by adults with a chlorine bleach solution (*1/4 cup bleach to one gallon water*).

Various types of *paper* can be used for countless fine motor activities, including cutting, drawing, painting, pasting, scrunching, sculpting, tearing and winding. That's why parents and other teachers often keep a supply of paper on hand for educational purposes. Coffee filters, construction paper, newsprint, paper napkins, and tissue paper are all useful for creative crafts.

A fringe snipped around a rolled paper cone resembles the petals of a flower when the edge of a dull knife is used to curl the petals. Paper dolls and snowflakes are more complicated projects that sometimes surprise us when we unfold them, just as written compositions often surprise us with new meaning when read aloud!

Children will be able to cut images from magazines more easily if the pictures they choose are first outlined in simple shapes. Circles, squares and triangles can be drawn by adults using a thick permanent marker. Arranged as a collage, pictures from magazines can be pasted on paper for wall decorations, or given as gifts to favorite friends and relatives. Making arrangements of pictures could be practice for making arrangements of *words*, which is what writers do.

Although television ads have supplanted many paper advertisements, colorful paper ads still entice consumers to buy specific products. Advertisements and coupons are delivered with my mail several days a week, and extra sections of coupons and ads come with my weekend newspaper. Aware of our fragile earth, wise parents and other teachers will recycle these ads for children's art.

Tissue paper balls make three-dimensional designs when they're pasted on cardboard, but dry pasta shapes can make a collage with a different bumpy texture. Young children who pick up individual pieces of pasta are exercising their pincer grips, which will be used to hold pencils and pens for writing. Six-year-olds can paste dry pasta over their names to create a textured sign, and beginning writers can compose messages and short poems using dry alphabet noodles pasted on heavy paper or poster board.

Non-toxic paste can be purchased in craft stores, drug stores, or grocery stores, but home-made paste can be mixed up from recipes below using common household ingredients.

UNCOOKED CRAFT PASTE

1 cup flour
½ cup water
Mix till creamy
Store in airtight container.

COOKED CRAFT PASTE

Boil 1 cup water
Add ½ cup flour
Reduce heat to low

Stir until thick and shiny
Allow to cool before use.

Japanese origami, the art of paper folding, involves coordinating hands and fingers and following sequential directions, skills needed for almost all art, including writing. The simplest origami projects can be completed by preschoolers. My daughter Linnet felt a real sense of accomplishment when she drank water from a tiny paper cup that she herself had folded, to take a drink of water from the classroom fountain. Her wise kindergarten teacher had given the children an origami project that they would never forget!

Six-year-olds can use finger paint to practice writing alphabet letters, numbers, names, and simple words. Children can experiment with knuckles, wrists, palms, fingernails, elbows and the backs of their hands. They can use swirly, vertical, horizontal and diagonal lines to compose patterns. If finger paint is smeared around on a cookie sheet or a plastic tray, cleanup is relatively easy under running water. Sometimes shaving cream can be used as 'finger paint' on tabletops for easy cleanup, but not with children who might touch their eyes. Shaving cream stings!

My daughter once enjoyed finger painting with leftover whipped cream that I brought home from a college event. I thought it wiser to use the whipped cream as an unusual art material, rather than having the sugary dessert around to contribute to tooth decay. Linnet spread the whipped cream all over her face, her hair and whole body, but a quick dip in a warm tub solved that problem.

Painting can involve large or small brushes, sponges, sticks, or straws as tools. Painting at an easel is a different experience from painting on a flat surface like a table, or using paint to print with sponges, blocks, or potatoes. Two children can paint opposite each other on an upright sheet of clear plastic like Plexiglas©, resulting in an experience with interactive composition. Tracking and attention to detail are two painting skills that will be needed for later reading and writing.

When clothing was manufactured at home, sewing was an important part of a girl's education. Embroidery, quilting, sewing, tapestry and weaving were both decorative and useful arts. Today, in an age of technology and mass marketing, these once-common experiences with fabric, needle and thread must be organized for children by thoughtful parents and other teachers.

Colorful pieces of yarn, one end stiffened with tape, make a good 'needle and thread' for young children. Stringing pasta or breakfast cereal having large enough holes can amuse children, and patterning can be practiced using different shapes or colors for stringing, providing experiences with simple composition. When children plan their patterns as drawings with crayons on paper, they are actually recording their thoughts, a precursor to writing!

Yarn or ribbon can be used to embroider on sewing cards. Colorful cardboard or wooden sewing cards can be purchased at toy stores, but homemade sewing cards can be devised using clean Styrofoam© trays. An adult pokes the tray with a knitting needle along permanent marker lines that can be drawn by a young child. Older children learn simple embroidery stitches using a large needle and thread on donated pieces of cloth. Eventually middle school students can learn to crochet, to knit, or to quilt using their more advanced fine motor skills and skills of sequential patterning, which will be important later for writing compositions.

Manipulatives are necessary for exercising fine motor skills. Look around your house or classroom. Do you see chalk, clay and dough, cereal shapes, crayons, dry rice and beans, markers, paint, paper, paste, pencils, sand, scissors, yarn, water toys, and a few commercial manipulatives, such as building toys and puzzles?

Commercially available manipulative toys like small building blocks, construction sets, nesting cups, pegs, puzzles and tools, can enhance children's eye-hand coordination. When treats are picked up one at a time with fingertips only, even snacks like raisins and dry cereal provide practice with the pincer grip. Any use of children's fine motor skills will benefit future writing, especially when practiced in a language-rich environment.

Get familiar with all the components of such a stimulating environment, but the most crucial aspect of the language environment is hearing books read aloud, which is very important for children to obtain the concepts and writing skills they'll need in school and later in their adult lives. Reading aloud is so important for speaking, reading, and writing that the next chapter is devoted to children's books, a critical element in the paper chain.

CHAPTER 2

Reading Aloud Leads to Lifelong Learning

IN HER AUTOBIOGRAPHY TITLED *ONE Writer's Beginnings*, author Eudora Welty remembered, "I learned from the age of two or three that any room in our house, at any time of day, was there to be read in, or to be read to."

Hearing books read aloud typically segues into reading on our own during the primary school years. But even after children can read on their own, they shouldn't always have to read alone. Older children like to hear chapter books read aloud in installments at bedtime. On road trips I still read aloud to my husband, making the miles seem shorter for both of us.

We often hear that reading aloud to children is important for their development, but exactly how does listening to a book help children learn? All caregivers of children, including their parents and other teachers, can use books in at least ten educational ways that will lead to lifelong learning *(Billboard E)*.

BILLBOARD E: Ten Educational Ways to Use Books

1. To entertain children,
2. To enhance language development,
3. To promote literacy,
4. As bibliotherapy,
5. To teach values,
6. To enrich multicultural understanding,
7. To increase knowledge,
8. To inspire creativity,

9.   As a management tool, and

10. To engage children in lifelong learning.

Often called *Story Time* or *Time for a Book,* this daily read-aloud can be introduced with a poem or a quiet song to set the mood for listening in classrooms and in bedrooms. As children become accustomed to this routine, they will begin to associate books with enjoyment. Parents and other teachers could make up a dreamy tune to carry the words to a reading song, or use a poem to introduce books.

A STORY TIME SONG

Time to draw near,
What shall we hear?
I'd like to read to you now.
Please choose a seat,
And let me repeat,
I'd LOVE to read to you now.

A POEM TO INTRODUCE BOOKS

When you open a book,
Certain things might fly out—
Things that can beckon,
And things that can shout.
When you open a book,
You might even be caught,
By a thing that you may not
Have known that you sought!

Good books are entertaining to children, so the *first* reason to read aloud is that children's books are just plain fun! Children will sit spellbound listening to a well-written story or poem, and they will beg for their favorites over and over. Read their favorite book again! When children *want* repetition, they probably *need* repetition to solidify their learning.

Resources like *Poems for Children: A Delightful Collection for Boys and Girls*, compiled by Kate James and illustrated with paintings by Jessie Willcox Smith, M. E. Gray and other artists, could inspire a true love of language, that quirky indulgence of all good writers. This collection of children's poetry was published in 1993 by Random House, but I was first inspired by *Poems of Early Childhood*, published by Childcraft in 1949. I read to my daughters from *Best Loved Nursery Rhymes and Songs*, published by Parents' Magazine Enterprises in 1974. Many collections of children's poetry are found on-line at www.alibris.com or in stores selling used books.

The entertainment value of good books is enhanced by enjoyable language. Consonance, alliteration, double meanings, clever plotting that includes suspense and surprise . . . All the tools of skillful writers help to hold a child's interest. For example, *The Piggy in the Puddle*, written by Charlotte Pomerantz and illustrated by James Marshall, is a book to tickle children with tongue twisting word play. In classics like *Green Eggs and Ham*, Theodor Geisel (pen name, Dr. Seuss) demonstrated that he was an earlier master of word play. For *The Cat in the Hat*, Dr. Seuss also devised a very clever plot. J. K. Rowling is a recent master of word play, using evocative names in her Harry Potter books, such as *Muggles, Hogwarts, Lucius Malfoy,* and *Slytherin.*

By increasing children's vocabulary and demonstrating a variety of grammatical structures, books can enhance language development in a first or a second language. That's the *second* reason to read books aloud. Context will provide clues to the meaning and usage of new vocabulary, so books can supplement everyday conversation and rote learning. By reading longer and longer novels, as well as poetry, plays, and informative nonfiction, older children continue to increase vocabulary and improve their grammar.

Historical romances like *Celia Garth* by Gwen Bristow, or *The Witch of Merthyn* by Richard Llewellyn, often touch on issues that continue to incite controversy in many countries, including the role of women in the modern world and the value of languages used by minorities. The classic novel *Ramona* by Helen Hunt Jackson, friend to Emily Dickinson, vividly describes the tragic mistreatment of native Californians as the United States expanded across the continent.

For younger children, author David A. Adler has published short picture book biographies of famous people, including Amelia Earhart, Lou Gehrig, Patrick Henry, Helen Keller, Rosa Parks, and more than fifty others. Older readers will be fascinated by books like *The Diary of a Young Girl* by Anne Frank and *An Autobiography* by Bill Peet, which peer into very different lives.

A number of classic children's books that were originally written in English are now available in Spanish, French, German, Russian, and other languages. At a time when they are biologically primed for language learning, young children will enjoy comparing written words in two or more languages. As they move through translations of familiar stories, older children will begin to read for meaning in a foreign language.

Find these translated classics in any bookstore with a good selection of children's books.

Dover Publications is one source of some very inexpensive foreign language books for children. *My First Hiragana Activity Book* by Yuko Green introduces simple words in Japanese. Hayward Cirker and Barbara Steadman created *Picture Word Books* for six different languages, including Hebrew and Italian. Each book offers line drawings of fifteen scenes with captions in a different language, and English translations of the word list. Order these books on-line, or send for the catalog at www.doverpublications.com.

Ruth Heller is an excellent English language vocabulary builder in her picture books, like *A Cache of Jewels and Other Collective Nouns*. In *The Year at Maple Hill Farm*, Alice and Martin Provensen also demonstrate interesting and varied grammar and provide rich information about animals, plants and people living in rural areas. Similes both common and rare are found in *Quick as a Cricket*, written by Audrey Wood and colorfully illustrated by Don Wood. Attractive books really enrich children's language learning.

As well as supporting oral language, reading books to children will teach pre-reading skills, the *third* reason to read aloud. The basic realization that marks on paper can represent spoken words is demonstrated in *dinner time* by Jan Pienkowski. The author pairs written animal names with pop-up pictures and a sequential story to dramatically demonstrate this literacy concept. Seven basic concepts to be grasped before real reading and writing begins are listed below in *Billboard F*.

BILLBOARD F: Seven Basic Concepts for Reading and Writing

1. Speech Can Be Written Down
2. Writing Can be Read
3. Most Adults Can Read
4. What's Read Can Be Spoken Aloud

5. Combinations of Specific Letters Stand for Words
6. Combinations of Words Stand for Whole Ideas
7. Specific Letter Order and Word Order Matter for Meaning

Children will be reassured that they share common human experiences with other people when they hear realistic stories read aloud. Books are comforting because they can be therapeutic, the *fourth* reason to read to youngsters. Children will soon recognize that storybook characters face situations similar to their own, and that well-developed characters find clever solutions to their problems.

In *Look at Me*, written by Charlotte Hall Ricks and illustrated by Annie Gusman, Catherine can't seem to get her busy mother's attention no matter how hard she tries.

Another protagonist experiments with running away from home in *A Baby Sister for Frances*, written by Russell Hoban, with pictures by Lillian Hoban. Almost all young children can identify with the temporary frustration experienced by these characters.

The *fifth* reason for reading to children also involves identification with characters in books. As children vicariously experience other people's lives, they learn about real-life values. They develop moral values they can use when faced with situations previously encountered by favorite characters in books.

Old age, death, and ongoing family relationships are explored in *Nana Upstairs and Nana Downstairs* by Tomie de Paola. The same subjects are treated in a different context when a family faces the death of a pet in *The Tenth Good Thing about Barney,* by Judith Viorst. In high quality books written for children, heavy topics will be handled with a light touch. For older children, *Good Night, Mr. Tom* by Michelle Magorian explores child abuse, and *Dreamland* by Sarah Dessen deals with a battering boyfriend.

Many novels are engrossing as they teach about history. *The Deserter: Murder at Gettysburg* is a Civil War mystery written by Jane Langton. *Fever 1793*, by Laurie Halse Anderson, takes place in Philadelphia after the Revolutionary War, during one of the worst epidemics in American history. *Out of the Dust* by Karen Hesse talks about personal and community tragedy in America during the 1930's. *Number the Stars* by Lois Lowry deals with Nazis in Denmark in World War II. Good novels can inspire educational conversations about weighty issues.

Books can enrich multicultural understanding, even when children live in a neighborhood where most people speak the same language. The *sixth* reason to read aloud is that whatever their ethnic background, children can feel, temporarily, just like the people in the story. This identification can increase empathy with people of different ages, or with those having different careers.

In *Everybody Cooks Rice*, written by Norah Dooley and illustrated by Peter J. Thornton, children discover that neighbors from Barbados, China, Haiti, India, Italy, Puerto Rico and Vietnam all have rice for dinner! In *Cleversticks*, written by Bernard Ashley and illustrated by Derke Brazell, Ling Sung discovers that his skill with chopsticks impresses the whole class. Chopsticks didn't play a role in our traditional Polish cuisine, but my daughter Linnet demonstrated the use of chopsticks for her second grade class! All the students loved *lo mein* noodles and vegetarian fried rice.

Ezra Jack Keats illustrated his charming stories like *The Snowy Day* with African-American children. In *A Chair for My Mother*, Vera B. Williams gives us a slice of city life. In *A Ride on Mother's Back*, illustrated by Durga Bernhard, Emery Bernhard tells how babies are carried in many different cultures around the world. My daughters listened attentively when I read *The Work People Do: Auto Mechanic*, so they could understand their father's workday. Your children might enjoy *Animal Doctor* in the same series, by author Betsy Imershein. Many children will relate to *Going to Day Care* by Fred Rogers. He gave us a glimpse of a child's and teacher's typical day in child care.

Mature readers will be interested in novels like *I Know Why the Caged Bird Sings* by Maya Angelou, about African Americans; *The Joy Luck Club* by Amy Tan, about

Chinese Americans; *Angela's Ashes: A Memoir* by Frank McCourt, about Irish Americans; *The Jew Store* by Stella Suberman, about Russian Americans; and *Hoopi Shoopi Donna* by Suzanne Stempek Shea, about Polish Americans. Through a variety of good books, children can enter our increasingly diverse society before they enter the global marketplace. With the current ease of travel and the worldwide connections made possible through telephone, e-mail, and web sites, today's children will probably be citizens of the globe when they grow up!

A book can increase general concept development and pre-academic knowledge. This learning can start children off on the right academic foot, the *seventh* reason to read aloud. If stories for children take place in other countries or in times past, they can introduce unfamiliar plants or animals, and illustrate different human cultures.

Some subtle tales of different places and times are *Caps for Sale: A Tale of a Peddler, Some Monkeys and Their Monkey Business*, told and illustrated by Esphyr Slobodkina; *Ming Lo Moves the Mountain* by Arnold Lobel; and *Whale in the Sky* by Anne Siberell. These bear re-reading as older children begin to understand the clever tricks played by the characters.

Other books clarify concepts like time, shape, number, sequence and size, in stories that have fascinated children for generations. *Millions of Cats* by Wanda Gag is an early picture book that still delights children with its repetitive refrain about huge numbers. *The Carrot Seed* by Ruth Krauss, with pictures by Crockett Johnson, tells a simple story of the patience needed to grow plants.

In *Swimmy* by Leo Lionni, soft paintings illustrate a hard lesson taught by the ocean. Staying together and working as a group can keep the small fish safe! You can't go wrong with any good alphabet book, but *A is for Aloha* by Stephanie Feeney, with photographs by Hella Hammid, offers a glimpse of life in Hawaii in striking photos. *V is for Volunteer: A Tennessee Alphabet* by Michael Shoulders is a close-up view of another state. *A is for Africa* by Ifeoma Onyefulu also uses photos to illustrate culture.

The Number 10 Duckling, written by Betty Rosendall and illustrated by Tom Dunnington, is a counting book based on a true story. What happens when a family of ducks visits a swimming pool owned by a human family? *Counting is for the Birds*, by Frank Mazzola, Jr. will intrigue young bird watchers. With a slightly scientific bent, *Counting Wildflowers* by Bruce McMillan also lets children practice counting to 20. In the appendix the author tells where and when to find beautiful common wildflowers.

Older children will learn about history when reading *Toys Through Time: How Toys Were Designed, Developed, and Made* by Chris Oxlade, or *Marguerite Makes a Book* by Bruce Robertson, about illuminated manuscripts. Dover Publications has books that both entertain and educate older children, including the *Cathedrals of the World Coloring Book* by John Green and *Castles of the World Coloring Book* by A. G. Smith.

The *eighth* reason to read aloud is for books to inspire children's own creativity. Starting with a good book, teachers and parents can use rhythm, movement, drawing, painting, drama, and song to increase language production and other kinds of expressive art. *Jamberry* by Bruce Degan can inspire all sorts of artistic responses and imitations with its jazzy text and dreamy illustrations. Creative thinking is also inspired by *A House Is a House for Me*, cleverly written by Mary Ann Hoberman and illustrated in complex detail by Betty Fraser. Older Children might be inspired to write poetry when they read *Nonsense Poems* by Edward Lear, or *A Light in the Attic* by Shel Silverstein.

Books also can be used as a management tool to control children's excitement, to aid in transitions, and to manage movement in the classroom or at home, which is the *ninth* reason to read aloud. "Let's sit down and listen to a story," a caregiver can say to calm the children, easing the transition to hand washing and table setting before lunch.

Goodnight Moon and *The Runaway Bunny*, both written by Margaret Wise Brown with pictures by Clement Hurd, can be very calming. But don't send children to the book corner as a punishment, and don't tell children to look at a book just so they'll be quiet and confined during transitions. You might unintentionally be sending the wrong message about reading! Books should be used primarily for enjoyment and learning, but only rarely to control young children's movements. On the other hand, older children may welcome the chance to relax with a good book or magazine, so have lots of reading matter available, as in a doctor's waiting room.

The *tenth* and most important use of reading aloud is to help adults engage children in the habit of lifelong learning. Even in our world of CDs, DVD's, the *Internet* and *Kindle*, some information is found only in real books and is most accessible through reading. You can read a book anywhere, on the bus or on the beach. Use Ruth Heller's entertaining science books, including *Chickens Aren't the Only Ones, Animals Born Alive and Well, The Reason for a Flower,* and *Plants That Never Ever Bloom,* to delight the emerging naturalist in every child. After older children have sampled the classic *Tales from Shakespeare* by Charles and Mary Lamb, they could be intrigued enough to tackle the Bard himself, as many students do in high school.

I've named some of my favorite children's books as examples of healthy reads. Almost all hese books are listed in *Appendix III, Selected Children's Books to Read Aloud.* As children mature, use *Appendix IV, Books for Older Children to Read.* Use these lists as a starting point to gather a collection of your own favorite children's books.

Take other suggestions from television programs on your public broadcasting channel, such as *Between the Lions* or *Reading Rainbow,* or at www.pbskids.org. The public library also carries free book lists to pick up next time you're looking for a good family read. With a book list, you can find plenty of books to order at www.amazon.com, or at www.alibris.com. A resource for very reasonably priced children's books is found at www.doverpublications.com. Try to support your neighborhood independent bookstores, or try Barnes & Noble Booksellers.

And don't forget the public library! Kindergartners really enjoy exploring those huge shelves of books. By the age of four many children can learn to selectively take books off a shelf and return them to appropriate bins to be re-shelved properly by librarians, or by volunteers like my daughter Julia, who loved to work among books.

Continue to buy sturdy hardback books for children to own, conveniently stored in their own little library on a bookshelf at home. Good books can be found on sales counters in many bookstores, so start a collection for your children. A shelf of books in a child's own bedroom or playroom, books to be looked at again and again whenever interest strikes, can promote a sense of belonging to the world of reading and writing. As a bonus, many children learn to use books at home with clean hands!

The children who develop a habit of finding good books on interesting subjects and reading them for pleasure are sure to become self-regulated learners. Adults who pick up books to read aloud to children are actually promoting the use of books for lifelong learning. Remember, according to biographies of famous authors like Agatha Christie and Eudora Welty, the children who fall in love with books at an early age often become the adults who write well. Check out my ten tips for reading aloud below, in *Billboard G.*

BILLBOARD G: Ten Tips for Reading Aloud

1. Young children can sit next to you, or in a small group as an audience.
2. Hold the book so children can view the cover easily.
3. Announce the title of the book while pointing to it. Read the names of author and illustrator (*Written by . . . Pictures by . . .*)
4. Read the book aloud slowly, clearly, and with animated expression.
5. Use voices for different characters that sound funny, scary, sad, high, deep . . .
6. At the end of each page, make a comment about the illustration or the action. (*She's so tall; That's a long snake; What a scary monster; A red balloon!*)

7. Don't be preachy or 'teachy' in your comments; Indicate wonder and interest.

8. Let a child turn the pages. (Say *Ready? Turn.*)

9. Ask simple questions of children (*Which kitten do you like? Where's the dog?*)

10. Ask questions that require thinking, not simple factual answers.
   (*How will they do that? Why do they want that? Where will they go?*)

CHAPTER 3

In Primary School from Six to Nine

READING ALOUD TO CHILDREN SHOULDN'T end after kindergarten! Children in primary school still love to have books read to them. Now they enjoy their favorite picture books as well as the new excitement of chapter books. Throughout elementary school, listening to books will continue to expand children's vocabulary and other language skills, laying a strong foundation for writing.

By primary school children are ready for new challenges. Many primary school children will have begun to read and write in kindergarten, absorbing lessons from the language-rich environment. Others will require reading and writing instruction customized to their own learning style and developmental schedule. For many children, the primary grades are the time to teach letter-sound correspondence and beginning blending of the sounds represented by the letters, while continuing to provide enriched experiences with many types of books (*Billboard H*).

BILLBOARD H: How to Enrich Reading Experience

- Rotate a variety of children's books that are accessible much of the day.
- Read *Big Books* aloud, pointing to the words as you say them.
- Read the same books again and again, until children can fill in missing words.
- Read a variety of stories and books aloud, including *adventure, alphabet, animals, biography, biology, classics, counting, crafting, fairy tales, fantasy, history, humor, mystery, nature, poetry, tradition, science, sports.*
- Read a book aloud to inspire a dance, art, gardening, or cooking project.

- Point to authors' and illustrators' names on the cover or title page.
- Give children hardbacks as presents to gradually fill their personal shelf of books.
- Make homemade books with children.
- Take children on a field trip to a school, a public library, or a bookstore.
- Take children's dictation as they explain their artwork or tell a story.
- Read children's words to them, demonstrating the purpose and value of writing.
- Have children illustrate their own stories or poems.
- Send children's stories and books to friends and family members.

I like to teach reading skills in a meaningful context, using the *Language Experience Approach*. The classic books *Spinster* and *Teacher,* written by Sylvia Ashton-Warner, were my introduction to the teaching methods this gifted teacher named *organic reading*. Ashton-Warner developed her use of *key vocabulary* with Maori children in New Zealand. Children's motivations and interests inspired Ashton-Warner's work, so she allowed young children to choose their own first words to read, such as *Mummy, Daddy, kiss,* and *ghost.* The children could easily remember these powerful words, because they were already part of the child's inner world.

Jeannette Veatch and her colleagues built upon Ashton-Warner's work in *Key Words to Reading: The Language Experience Approach Begins.* Judith Schickedanz updates this child-oriented approach in *Much More than ABC's: The Early Stages of Reading and Writing.* Schickedanz cites research on literacy, and offers practical suggestions like lists of books and materials to use at learning centers in modern classrooms. These methods are especially important if children have not worked with preschool and kindergarten teachers who had an excellent understanding of child development.

Using the *Key Word* approach, adults invite children to name a word they would like to add to their stock of personal key words. The children begin to collect key vocabulary on index cards stored in plastic file boxes, or on large metal rings that can be carried like a key ring. Both storage methods have disadvantages. File boxes can be dropped so all the cards scatter, but key rings are hard for small hands to open and close. A composition book can be used instead. With grown-up help, children can create a personal dictionary by placing letters of the alphabet as headings on individual pages, and listing words that start with that letter below the heading.

The formal study of *phonics* has a place in primary school, when children range in age from about six to nine. English, however, is a language full of irregularity, so the rules of phonics have limited utility. To learn more about our language, adults will enjoy *The Mother Tongue: English and How It Got That Way* and *Made in America: An Informal History of the English Language in the United States,* by scholarly humorist Bill Bryson.

When children are beginning to read and write, concentrate on the regular patterns found in simple words of one syllable. Repetition can help children learn to read these words by sight. Choose words that sound similar, such as *mad, man, map, mask, mast,* and *mat.* Slowly read your short word list to a child.

When children can repeat this list while pointing to each word, create a silly sentence to read using most of those words. For example, *A mad man in a mask sat on a mat with a map.* Have props on hand, such as a *map* and a *mask,* so children can act out the silly sentence. Then write that sentence on the bottom of a piece of paper, so it can be illustrated with a drawing or a collage.

Be sure the artwork is signed or initialed before hanging a child's drawing on a refrigerator or bulletin board. Ask your child to read the caption aloud throughout the day, until reading those words becomes automatic. When you're working with first words to be read by children, try other silly sentences, such as *Hal had a ham in his hand, not on his hat; On a dull day Deb sat at her desk on the deck;* or *Jill did a jig with a pig, not a cat or a rat.*

As children start to learn about phonics, most won't need many more lessons, because they'll pick up the rest of the more complicated rules on their own. Human brains are expert at extracting the rules of language from a language-rich environment. Once children have become real readers, exposure to more and more words written by competent authors will do the rest. In other words, children really need to hear books read aloud! Typical schooling will soon fill in any gaps in a child's knowledge of phonics.

Primary school is the time to purchase a simple dictionary for children. Alphabetizing is a new, challenging, and practical skill to conquer. *My Honey Bear Picture Word Book,* compiled by Lynne J. Bradbury and illustrated by Lynn N. Grundy is a fine first dictionary. Angela Wilkes and Rubí Borgia offer *mi primer libro de palabras en español* with wonderful photographs of Spanish vocabulary items.

Word-find puzzles and crossword puzzles can be assembled using children's own key words. Games like *Word Scramble* can be played at home or in a classroom. Can children find a specific word when several key word cards are scrambled on the floor or on a table? Can children find words that rhyme with *fat*? A word that means the opposite of *down*? A word for an animal that lives with people in their houses? Is it *frog, hog,* or *dog*?

As children begin to recognize simple words, they can read whole books written especially for their age group. Called *Easy Readers* or *Easy-to-Read*, these books have controlled vocabulary that can be recognized as sight words, or sounded out with beginning phonics by the children themselves. The hilarious and touching series about *Frog and Toad* by Arnold Lobel and the classic *Green Eggs and Ham* by Dr. Seuss are two easy reads that will be fondly remembered. Many easy reads are available in bookstores or on-line, and there are hundreds more at your local public library.

Children will be very excited when they can read these books aloud to an adult: a bit of turnabout! But reading is supposed to be fun, so don't let children struggle to read any words that give them trouble. Just audibly fill in the word and move on. Maybe you can take turns reading pages aloud. You'll find some books designed exactly for this purpose in any good bookstore that sells children's books.

In primary school the connections between visual art and writing become more obvious. Now adults can take dictation from children for labels, signs, and stories, and the children will be more interested in creating illustrations for these than ever before. When children have intriguing new tools like colored pens or markers, and several different kinds of paper, they can be inspired to write on their own.

Young children can create signs, greeting cards, letters, poems, and small books. Diaries and journals are gifts that might be appreciated by older children as they learn to write in primary school. The arts of *collage* and *journal keeping* will begin to interest some children in primary school, but these activities will really become successful during middle school.

Knowledge of the alphabet is very useful in primary school, so each child should have at hand a personal chart of the alphabet letters, and numerals from one to ten. Several laminated charts can be taped to tables throughout the primary classroom and on small desks at home. Alphabet charts should be created in simple, legible fonts. Labels, lists, and notes typed in easy-to-read fonts will support new readers and writers. Computer word processing software will offer a variety of very legible fonts to use, preferably in size 12-point or higher.

Teaching children manuscript is a wonderful gift you can offer to them, but don't make writing practice tedious or dull. Educational research demonstrates that when children are interested in any activity, they're learning more as they perform that activity. It sounds counter-intuitive, but when writing practice is a chore, children are not learning as effectively as they could be. Don't be fooled into thinking that learning should be hard. Remember that children develop at different rates, so some children will begin to write earlier, and some a little later. In child development, faster is not better!

My older daughter came home crying when her first grade teacher began to reward children for the nicest handwriting. "If only she gave out pencils or something, instead of a bag of candy," wailed my six-year-old. Linnet was not an early reader or writer. Sadly, in first grade she knew that she'd never win a bag of chocolates for good handwriting. But now she's a college graduate who writes for a living, and, like most professionals, she types with a computer more often than she writes by hand! Who cares how well she printed her letters at six-years-old?

I like to start young children with printing using the D'Nealian alphabet, but there are other systems that are equally good for beginning writers. Ask your child's teacher what your school recommends. When you type for children, whether you're creating a shopping list or you're privately publishing children's poetry, use a clear, simple font in a fairly large size.

A book like *How Our Alphabet Grew* by William Dugan makes a good resource for both teachers and students. Children will enjoy learning some fascinating facts about the history of writing and printing. Did you know that Rome's first public library was opened by Asinius Pollio back in 30 BC? That the first book was printed in China in 868 A.D. and that Johannes Gutenberg invented movable type in Europe in 1454? That the alphabet as we know it was passed from the Phoenicians, to the Greeks, to the Romans? Children may appreciate writing more when they understand that books didn't always exist.

Frequently suggest but *don't demand* that children draw, paint, or write. As in so many endeavors, improvement comes with experience. Writing exercises like those detailed in Chapter 8 will encourage children's independent writing. Arranged by level of difficulty, the exercises are designed to strengthen young writers. To keep children's motivation high, it's important to offer choices in writing exercises, but don't overwhelm a child with too many choices! The products of children's efforts can be displayed or self-published, letting children know that they are already writers!

Continue to visit libraries and bookstores. There the children can choose books, experience *readings*, and meet published authors in person. Any contact with authors can inspire new writers, but did you know that by *cooking* with children we help them become good writers, as well as real cooks? When I was a classroom teacher I named one themed unit *We Cook with a Book*, a unit that revolved around stories for children that featured food, like *Popcorn* by Frank Asch.

Children experience their world in a less categorized way than adults, so an *integrated curriculum* is a developmentally appropriate way to teach children. Cooking activities are suitable for any integrated curriculum and, in fact, cooking can provide the theme itself! Under one theme all the typical school subjects can be addressed in an integrated day.

All young children learn in a more global way than older children and adults learn. Young children's brains are not yet fully differentiated, so they seem to absorb and practice new information using several senses at once. Cooking is an ideal multi-sensory activity, involving more than the familiar five senses. That's why well planned cooking activities, which include preparing simple cold foods like fruit, can lead to good eating and to improved reading and writing skills.

When children are in primary school, their parents and other teachers can use cooking experiences to promote the basic skills involved in reading and writing. Cooking activities provide learning opportunities for children who are typically developing, for children with special needs, and for children with precocious development. For this reason, cooking has long been a standard activity in early childhood classrooms.

I started cooking with children in school in the 1970s, when I was an undergraduate *Participant* in an open primary classroom. Now I am struck by how few modern classrooms include adequate space, equipment, or materials for cooking activities with children. Our increased awareness of the important role of cleanliness for children's health is partially responsible for this shift, but something of value has been lost.

Here the home-school teacher has an advantage, because a family kitchen can be a perfect place to cook up basic skills, along with delicious recipes. Parents and other teachers can use cooking to pursue educational goals for children, including their reading and writing skills. Educators advocate curricula based on experiential, multi-sensory, and language-based approaches to instruction, and a kitchen is perfect for these approaches!

Numerous resources on nutrition, like the references at the end of this chapter, have recipes and methods suitable for children. But here we're more concerned with the *why* than with the *how* of cooking. Even experienced classroom chefs might not understand the full educational value of cooking.

Being fed, and being able to feed one's self and others, are associated with the basic need for survival, so children will become fully involved in a lesson that involves food. Cooking real food to be eaten by their family and friends is a real-life experience, which is appreciated by most children. Cooking is seen as an adult task, having high value in a child's mind. Any opportunity to act like a grown-up can be motivating to children.

Cooking activities can also inspire involvement by family members who are willing to share, say, their salad-making skills. Parents and children from the neighborhood can join you when you're baking bread, cookies, pies and casseroles, or when you're concocting a fruit salad. Of course, you'll let them take some samples home!

A mother born in Ireland once demonstrated baking soda bread to my kindergarten class. Families from other cultural backgrounds could share pasta, tacos, rice noodles, pierogies, cheese grits, or okra. Most families are happy to offer a vegetable for *Stone Soup*, a recipe based on a folk tale. Because I combined learning with cooking when I was a teacher, my kindergarten classroom was well known for its enticing odors!

All young children need to practice *self-help skills*. Some children with special needs may be a little behind their peers in tasks like hand washing, nose wiping, dressing, or eating with utensils. Cooking provides many opportunities to practice these self-help skills in a meaningful context. For example, smocks or aprons are buttoned or tied, and both our hands and vegetables are well scrubbed before cooking.

The concepts and skills gained in cooking activities are highly practical, as well as quite adaptive. They range from mathematics and chemistry to proper hygiene. The skills practiced by young cooks can be generalized to a variety of environments, from family homes to employment opportunities as different as a hospital laboratory or a restaurant kitchen. Both my brother, a chef, and my husband, a mechanic, use visual-motor skills children can practice as they cook!

Organizational problems are associated with many learning difficulties. Cooking activities have an inherent logical order that can help teach principles of organization. For example, for baking we mix the dry and wet ingredients separately. Without yeast the bread won't rise, and for soup we need spoons, not forks.

The principles of mathematical logic are also observable at the table. One-to-one correspondence, a concept necessary for mathematics, is apparent as we place one plate in front of each chair, one napkin by each plate, and one fork on each napkin. Fractions are demonstrated when we cut up one apple to give three people a snack. Two half cups equal the whole cup called for in a recipe.

Cooking activities have an inherent temporal sequence. We must set the table before we serve the spaghetti, boil the water before we add the gelatin, and cook the potatoes before we mash them. These seemingly simple examples of logic can underpin a child's later, more sophisticated, learning. A curriculum based on cooking will lend itself to that touchstone of high quality education, a hands-on approach. *Children learn by doing!* Few activities require so much doing, from *Adding* salt to soup to *Zapping* food in a microwave oven, as illustrated by *The ABC's of Cooking,* in Billboard I, below.

Children with disabilities need hands-on lessons as much as, or more than, typically developing children. Some children require motor stimulation to concentrate, and some children who seem constantly on the move need to have their movements channeled in positive ways. All young children, however, will listen more attentively to a lesson while they're kneading dough or stirring pudding.

Hands-on cooking activities can encourage the development of fine motor control and strength, skills required for writing. For children who don't have mature physical development, many so-called prewriting activities, including the highly structured tracing of alphabet letters, can prove frustrating. Unfortunately, this early frustration might lead to academic avoidance later on.

A developmentally appropriate alternative would be to orchestrate cooking activities that build strength and control in parts of the body involved in writing. These include the *trunk, neck, shoulders, upper arms, wrists,* and *fingers*. One child can benefit from rolling out cookie dough, building strength in upper arms and wrists, while another child can use clean scissors to cut cookies from rolled dough, working on control and strength of the fingers. Children with mature motor skills can feel proud as they help their classmates.

For optimal learning, children require new information to be presented through more than one sensory channel at a time. In a *multi-sensory approach* one learning mode can reinforce another mode, and sometimes a stronger sense can compensate for a weaker one. What is referred to as *sensory integration deficit* in some children can be treated with therapeutic activities involving more than one sensory channel at a time.

Children whose auditory processing is still developing may be led through cooking activities using their stronger visual skills. Meanwhile, as the adult comments on everything a child can see, the child's auditory channel is being strengthened. The sound of the first corn kernel popping is a wonderful reward for practicing good listening!

Children benefit from attaching the vocabulary of the tactile sense to real objects like a *prickly* pineapple, a *bumpy* avocado, or *slimy* egg whites. Some children with tactile defensiveness can be desensitized through a series of increasingly more tactilely rich experiences. They'll progress from slicing firm cheese to kneading the egg, tomato sauce, grated Parmesan cheese and breadcrumbs into the tofu. After this mixture is baked as a loaf, the children will want to slice and taste their delicious finished product.

The olfactory sense is known to be richly evocative, triggering long-stored memories. A wise adult takes advantage of this human tendency by occasionally attaching lessons in mathematics, science, phonics or social studies to a strong smell. Sorting raw onion rings by size, or counting separate garlic cloves, might be appropriate academic activities for a child who doesn't find these odors too unpleasant.

The gustatory sense is a powerful teaching agent. My daughter Julia read the words *Pizza Hut* very early because she associated the environmental print at her favorite fast food restaurant with her gustatory sense. Pizza was so yummy! Other children might read *Arby's, Bojangles, Hardee's, Kentucky Fried Chicken, McDonald's, Subway, Taco Bell,* or *Wendy's,* if fast food is a special treat for them.

BILLBOARD I: The ABC's of Cooking

ACTIONS	FOODS
Adding	Almonds, apples
Beating	Beans, bread
Cooling, cutting	Cheese, corn
Dipping, dissolving	Dates, dill pickles
Eating, enjoying	Eggs, enchiladas
Flipping, forming	Fish, fruit
Garnishing, grating	Garlic, grapes, grits
Halving, heating	Hamburger, honey
Icing	Ices, ice cream
Juicing	Jam, jelly, juice
Kneading	Kale, kasha
Licking	Lasagna, lemonade
Measuring, melting	Milk, macaroni, meat
Nourishing	Noodles, nuts
Oiling	Olives, oranges
Paring, pouring	Pancakes, potatoes
Quartering	Quiche, quick breads
Rolling out	Raisins, rice
Spreading, stirring	Soup, spices
Tasting, topping	Tofu, tortillas
Uncapping, uncovering	Ugli fruit
Valuing, varying	Vegetables, vanilla
Warming, whisking	Waffles, won tons
Xeroxing© (a recipe)	Xmas cookies
X-ing (venting a pie crust)	LoX and Bagels
Yanking, yelping (if food's too hot)	Yams, yogurt
Zapping (in a microwave oven)	Zucchini, ziti

Cooking activities take advantage of a powerful natural teaching tool. Squeezing some *lemons for lemonade*, or just having a *little lick of lemon*, can fix the sound of the letter L in a child's memory.

Functional vision, for example, is enhanced when looking has a real purpose. Children look closely to discover the moment water starts to boil, or to describe this strange object, a coconut. Then they watch carefully as an adult records their words, "It's hairy," on a language experience chart.

The ability to perceive hot and cold temperatures, sometimes referred to as the *thermic* sense, can be a possible lifesaver! For their own safety children should be taught to respect all objects that give off heat. Because the thermic sense is so often neglected in school, an adult's conscious use of varying temperatures can trigger close attention in children. Counting ice cubes or warm baked potatoes, for example, will be more memorable than counting plastic tokens.

The sense that enables perception of our own movements, which is located in our muscles, joints, and tendons, is called *kinesthesia*. Along with the tactile sense, kinesthesia can be enlisted to teach many basic concepts. Forming a letter in pretzel dough, for example, can fix the shape of a letter in a child's mind in a scrumptious way!

Children with physical disabilities, or children who are just a little clumsy, need special movement activities to develop adequate kinesthesia. Weight bearing of the upper extremities can be practiced while kneading or rolling out dough. Sometimes a change in body position, such as watching the popcorn popper while lying on the floor, chins propped on hands, or stirring a gelatin mixture while draped over a bolster, can be highly therapeutic for children with special needs. A physical or occupational therapist can recommend individualized body postures and positions.

The sense of time passing can be called the *temporal* sense. Children frequently lose track of time, but cooking activities can draw meaningful attention to time passing. A grown-up can say *Let's look at the hands on the clock. How long must the bread rise?*

What happens if we leave the rolls in the oven too long? How long must we wait for the paper cups of fruit juice to freeze?

By using a multi-sensory approach, we provide many hooks on which to hang new concepts or skills. In this way we can help children remember our lessons. Discoveries from the field of neurobiology support a multi-sensory and integrated approach to learning about concepts, over more fragmented teaching of individual discrete facts.

Patterns are better stored in long-term memory when they are associated in time. If meaningful experiences have been perceived almost simultaneously, they tend to be better remembered. Memory patterns might be retrieved when awareness of a small piece triggers awareness of the whole pattern. The author Marcel Proust famously reminded his readers of this fact in his novel, *Remembrance of Things Past*. A pastry madeleine evoked strong memories of childhood for Proust. Which smells do this for you? Grilled cheese on toast? Pizza sauce? Boiled cabbage? Banana bread baking?

During cooking activities grown-ups should ask questions that provoke children's thinking: *What is steam? What happens when water is cooled or heated? Will flavored gelatin get as hard as an ice cube when it's chilled? Will fruit juice freeze?* If children's attention is drawn to observable phenomena, eventually they will be fascinated by the *science* of cooking. Read the unit plan below as an example of a well-rounded learning experience. Use every opportunity to stress the target alphabet letters and sounds!

SAMPLE UNIT PLAN OUTLINE
To Introduce Alphabet Letters P and W

GOALS

The purpose of this unit is
- To introduce the visual and auditory characteristics of two letters of the alphabet
- To provide developmentally appropriate practice for later reading and writing

OBJECTIVES

At the end of this unit, children will
- Point as requested to letters p and w when 10 letters are shown
- Verbally identify letters p and w when 10 letters are shown
- Write letters p and w so they're recognizable to adults
- Name 5 words that start with p and w (*pow, wow, pan, wag, pie, why*)
- Enjoy language play with rhyming words (*pet, wet, pig, wig, pink, wink*)

ACTIVITIES

Throughout this unit, teachers will
- Offer several activities to enhance each domain of development
- Stress the sounds of beginning letters when listing activities
- Write the names of activities on signs and blackboards
- Draw attention to written letters p and w
- Repeat unit activities as often as children express interest

In this unit plan, cover every area of children's development using books, games, movies, objects, pictures, poems, and songs, and emphasize every P and W.

SUGGESTED ALPHABET ACTIVITIES

Sensory Perception

1. Water play, painting with brushes using water or water color paints
2. Playing Look-See games like Where's Waldo? Where's White?
3. Listening to popcorn pop
4. Preparing preferred foods like pretzels, pie, popcorn or pizza
5. Preparing prickly pineapples, peanut butter play dough, won ton noodles . . .

Gross Motor Skills

1. Moving like different animals, such as prancing horses or wiggling snakes
2. Using wheeled toys
3. Running with the wind using whirligigs
4. Participating in parachute play
5. Whacking piñatas

Fine Motor Skills

1. Tracing, coloring, and cutting whirligigs
2. Pasting pink and purple pictures
3. Cutting and weaving strips of paper for place mats

4. Wrapping packages for presents
5. Printing with potatoes (or wet sponges) and paint

Cognitive Skills

1. Observing popcorn changing as it's heated
2. Looking at spider webs (in pictures, or find a real web)
3. Playing with puppets
4. Completing wooden puzzles
5. Watching a movie about whales like *Free Willy*, or about pigs like *Babe*

Language Skills

1. Singing songs that emphasize p and w (examples below)
2. Hearing stories that emphasize p and w (examples below)
3. Reading poetry, or watching birds and squirrels
4. Writing short Wonder Poems
5. Dictating or recording sights seen on a Watching Walk

Social and Emotional Skills

1. Waiting for a turn with wheeled toys, a swing, or a bat
2. Waving at wizards and witches in the window (see song below)
3. Creating We Wish You Well cards for family and friends
4. Caring for a class pet: petting, providing water and food
5. Discussing Why I Am Proud

WELCOME TO W SONG (Melody *Cabaret*)

Welcome to W, Welcome!
Wonder what we will do, Welcome!
We wish for wizards and witches who will,
Wave at our window to give us a thrill.
Welcome to U and U, Welcome!
To W week, to W week, to W week.

I'M A LITTLE POPCORN (Melody *I'm a Little Teapot*)

I'm a little popcorn in a pot,
Heat me up and watch me pop.
When I get all fat and white I'm done.
Popping corn is lots of fun!
Pop! Pop! Pop! Pop! (Children spring up, shouting *Pop!*)

PEASE PORRIDGE HOT

Pease Porridge hot,
Pease Porridge cold,
Pease Porridge in the pot,
Nine days old!
Some like it hot,
Some like it cold,
Some like it in the pot,
Nine days old!

MIX A PANCAKE by Christina Rossetti

Mix a pancake,
Stir a pancake,
Pop it in the pan;

Fry the pancake,
Toss the pancake—
Catch it if you can.

Sing P and W songs:

Itsy Bitsy Spider Went up the Water Spout
My Little Puppy's Name is Rags
Oh, Where, Oh Where Has My Little Dog Gone?
The People on the Bus
Picking Up Paw-Paws

43

Read P and W Books:

Be Nice to Spiders by Margaret Bloy Graham
Piggy in the Puddle by Charlotte Pomerantz
Pretzel by Margret Rey
Where's Spot? by Eric Hill
Where The Wild Things Are by Maurice Sendak

Applesauce, potato pancakes, scrambled eggs, vegetable soup, and cookies are just a few foods mentioned in children's books. Use the list below, *Twelve Children's Books Featuring Food*, or ask your librarian to suggest other children's stories that refer to food. Small appliances such as an electric skillet or a toaster oven could allow children to observe the cooking closely, but explain and enforce sensible safety rules when cooking with children!

Within an integrated curriculum, *Social Studies* can revolve around the relationships of farms to cities. Children love big trucks and trains, so they'll enjoy the study of *Geography*, learning where the climate can support various food crops, and how crops are transported to processing plants and to market. The counting and measuring that's needed to follow a recipe, or to graph a taste test, involves *Mathematics*.

Hands-on *Science* learning can be the kitchen chemistry required to cook food safely, to dissolve gelatin, or to germinate sprouts in a jar. Dancing to appropriate ethnic music like a polka for pierogi, the *Mexican Hat Dance* for guacamole, or *Chanukah, Oh Chanukah* for potato latkes could be the physical education lesson that day.

Activities like listening to the story or poem that inspires cooking; recording observations, taste tests, and recipes on language experience charts; waiting to listen for instructions on cleaning and cooking food; discussing the results of cooking experiments; conversing with friends and teachers at the table; writing poems, songs or stories about meals or food . . . These are all part of an expansive *Language Arts* curriculum.

BILLBOARD J: TWELVE CHILDREN'S BOOKS THAT FEATURE FOOD

1. *Bread and Jam for Frances* by Russell Hoban, 1993
2. *Bread, Bread, Bread* by Ann Morris, 1989
3. *The Carrot Seed* by Ruth Krauss, 1945

4. *Everybody Cooks Rice* by Norah Dooley, 1991

5. *The Fruit 'N Food* by Leonard Chang, 2010

6. *The Gingerbread Boy* as retold by Richard Egielski, 1997

7. *Green Eggs and Ham* by Dr. Seuss, 1960

8. *How to Make an Apple Pie and See the World*, Marjorie Priceman (1994)

9. *Jamberry* by Bruce Degen, 1983

10. *Pancakes Pancakes* by Eric Carle, 1991

11. *Popcorn* by Frank Asch, 1979

12. *Stone Soup* by Marcia Brown, 1986

Cooking, like the other arts, lends itself to a process approach to learning. Yes, there is a worthwhile product (unless, of course, we burn it) but the process itself both fascinates and educates children. Cooking is exciting when approached with a scientific mindset. Or should we call it a *playful* mindset?

Predictions are made: How many seeds will this big avocado have?

Hypotheses generated: If we heat the corn kernels, they will turn black.

Experiments designed: Plain yogurt or cottage cheese in mashed potatoes?

Observations recorded: Cooked macaroni is larger than uncooked.

Questions raised: Why is this noodle bigger?

A *process approach* to curriculum relies on the principles of cause and effect. Young children might have difficulty understanding the effects of their actions, but cooking provides many chances to prove to children that what they do really matters. When we plan an emergent curriculum that grows out of children's interests, we should be alert to the children's ideas and to situations that lend themselves to a cooking activity. With gentle adult guidance, children will soon create interesting new recipes on their own!

Because cooking requires careful preparation, parents and other teachers will make plans to have the needed equipment and ingredients on hand. Some staples, such as peanut butter, honey, dry milk and cereal, can be pulled out at a moment's notice and used in several creative ways. Have you made peanut butter play dough recently? Here's a recipe that succeeded many times at home and in classrooms. You can copy this recipe on an index card or send copies home in your parent newsletter, but before you serve peanut butter at school, check with parents about children's allergies!

PEANUT BUTTER PLAY DOUGH

2 cups peanut butter
2 cups dry (powdered) milk
1 cup honey
(A little dry breakfast cereal is optional for crunch)
Mix, mold, refrigerate and enjoy!

Skilled teachers are aware of the many differences among children, so they'll design a flexible program matched to children's needs. Cooking activities are often suitable in responsive, individualized programs like tutoring or home schooling, as well as in classrooms integrated by age or ability, because *cooking invites flexibility!* Children will flourish in such flexible programs because they often exhibit strengths and weaknesses scattered across domains of ability.

Cooking activities can take place in an adult-directed, adult-facilitated, or child-directed manner. Food can be prepared on a picnic table or in a fancy modern kitchen. Varying levels of ability can be accommodated, making teaching through cooking ideal for family homes, or wherever children of various ages learn together.

When they cook, children with superior language skills can read the recipe. A child with developing motor skills can hold the bowl while someone else mixes. Many children do their best learning through a multi-sensory and hands-on approach, and children make more sense of an integrated curriculum and of a process approach than they do of a more fragmented or rote approach to learning. While they cook, the children can be learning practical and adaptive skills associated with organization and common sense, and with the basic principles of logic.

When you cook with children, you really can help them become writers, but always check your records for food allergies, and remind your young chefs to wash their hands with soap before they begin to cook. Because cooking is motivating, nurturing, and grounded in reality, all children can feel challenged and useful during cooking activities.

COOKING WITH PIZZAZ

I took a look,
Inside a book.
A recipe!

Now we can cook.
Wash your hands,
And gather your tools.
Recipes work,
When you follow the rules.

FOUR REFERENCES ON COOKING WITH CHILDREN

1. Aronson, S. (2002) *Healthy Young Children: A Manual for Programs,*
    National Association for the Education of Young Children
2. Bredekamp, S., & Copple, C. (1997) *Developmentally Appropriate Practice in Early Childhood Programs,* National Association for the Education of Young Children
3. Goodwin, M., & Pollen, G. (1980) *Creative Food Experiences for Children,*
    Center for Science in the Public Interest
4. Wilkes, A. (2001) *The Children's Step-by Step Cookbook.*
    Dorling Kindersley Publishing

CHAPTER 4

In Middle School from Ten to Thirteen

TYPICALLY, MIDDLE SCHOOL STUDENTS ARE entering that magical realm of double digits, ages 10 to 13. They tend to be more realistic in their understanding of the world than younger children, but they are not yet thinking like adults!

Adolescents are often self-aware and self-conscious, feeling like the center of attention. They're uncomfortable as they concentrate on their weight gain, muscle development, secondary sex characteristics, and changes in their complexions. Because adolescents tend to put a negative spin on their physical changes, the adults around them should try to focus on the positive. Reading and writing often provide excellent opportunities for sensible grown-ups to support sensational kids in middle school.

Most middle school children are stepping out, reaching beyond home, family, and school, so these are the years to point them to interesting newspaper and magazine articles. Many children use computers now, but they might need help finding appropriate websites to visit. The contact information below highlights some good resources.

MAGAZINES FOR YOUNG READERS AND WRITERS

SPIDER Magazine for Kids ages 6-9
CRICKET Magazine for Kids ages 9-14
Carus Publishing Company www.Cricketmag.com
1-800-821-0115

CREATIVE KIDS Magazine for Kids ages 8-14
Prufrock Press, Inc. (gifted, advanced, special needs learners)
www.prufrock.com
1-800-998-2208

NEW MOON GIRLS Magazine for Girls ages 8-12
Nancy Gruver, Founder
www.newmoon.com
1-800-381-4743

SKIPPING STONES Multicultural Magazine for ages 7-17
Arun Narayan Toké, Publisher and Editor
www.skippingstones.org
541-342-4956

TEEN VOICES Magazine for teen girls
Jessica Moore, Publisher and Editor
www.teenvoices.com
617-426-5505

KidPub Press for readers and writers ages 8-15
Perry Donham, Publisher
www.info@kidpub.com
1-800-252-5224

ZuZu
Restless Youth Press
Beth Underwood, Founder
www.zuzu.org

The right gifts for children include gifts that can improve their reading and writing skills. Books containing puzzles, such as *crosswords, acrostics* and *word finds,* make good gifts for children in middle school. By this age, most students are able to enjoy reading chapter books on their own. They're pleased to receive currently popular young adult novels, along with occasional magazines, comic books and, surprisingly, reference books!

Ambrogio Calepino in Italy published the first known dictionary in 1502. Now every modern family can have a big hardback dictionary to refer to when they play *Scrabble!* But a paperback dictionary or thesaurus also makes a good present for middle schoolers. Any reference book will seem like a grown-up gift, the opposite of dreaded *babyish* gifts.

Dictionaries are gifts that will be used frequently as children complete assignments for school, or read challenging books for pleasure. Some curious children, however, want their own *encyclopedia*, a broad collection of information about people, places and things, which goes beyond the facts contained in dictionaries. The first encyclopedia was published much earlier than any dictionary, by Pliny the Elder in Rome in 77 AD. Wise parents won't feel pressure to buy an expensive encyclopedia because public libraries buy new encyclopedias frequently, and those will be accessible and up-to-date.

The habit of keeping a diary or journal often develops in the middle school years, so attractive *blank books* make good presents for adolescents. Encouraging students' writing and drawing, blank books offer valuable practice in representation. Fancy tools for writing and the visual arts, such as glitter pens, markers of brilliant or unusual colors, glue sticks, stencils, stickers, watercolors, and pastels (colored chalks), make good gifts when children are mature enough to use these materials safely.

As children begin to think abstractly, the art of *collage* might be intriguing to them. Webster's dictionary defines collage as an artistic composition of objects and materials pasted over a surface, often with unifying lines and color. Collage is defined broadly, leaving lots of room for individual tastes.

In middle school our daughter Julia came to love collage so much that she covered the walls of her bedroom with pictures and text. Some images were cut from magazines, some from ads that came in the mail, and some from postcards or greeting cards. At age twelve Julia published an article about collage in *Dream Girl*, a local magazine.

> *A collage can be many things. It can be pictures, cloth, wood, tinfoil, paintings, duct tape (one of my favorites) . . . Decide how you want it to look, how you want the theme to be, and what sorts of things you're going to have in it. For instance, if you're interested in sports, you could decide to put up pictures of soccer balls, famous baseball players, people canoeing, or photos of you playing whatever kind of sport you play . . .*

> *Making collage is fun because you can just go up to your wall whenever you want and stick a picture up there. Of course, the main obstacle to this form of collage is getting your parents to let you. I started mine on a piece of paper and promised my parents that I would never go off it . . . Unfortunately, or rather, fortunately, I did. And my parents, though they aren't too happy, don't mind that much . . .*

Quilting is another art for teens to try in middle school. Quilting is a visual art that uses skills of composition, including brainstorming, recognizing themes, connecting and contrasting related ideas, and bringing closure to big projects. For some adolescent students, *acting* is a preferred form of representation, and for some young writers *play-writing* becomes an interest. To support children's creativity, school literary magazines can publish short plays, poetry, essays, and graphics like cartoons or border designs.

Cartooning is an art that takes off in middle school because it relies on *abstract thinking*, often demonstrated by adolescents. A cartoon is a recognizable representation of a person or object, but cartoons have some exaggerated features that express an identifying characteristic of the subject. Famous cartoonists like Charles Schultz (*Charlie Brown*) and Jim Davis (*Garfield*) became popular for writing, as much as for their drawing skills.

When you gather pieces for your school literary magazine, writing prompts will trigger ideas for poems, essays, and stories, especially if a choice of assignments is offered to the students. For example, ask children to describe in writing either an article of clothing that they never want to wear, or the article of clothing they wish they could wear every day.

The hilarious, irreverent poetry of Shel Silverstein delights middle schoolers. In *Runny Babbit: A Billy Sook* (Silverstein's last, and possibly, his silliest book) the poet strengthens children's phonics and reading skills by reversing beginning consonants, the *rirty dat*.

Two kinds of formal poetry that appeal to middle schoolers are the *limerick* and the *Japanese haiku*. Both require abstract thinking to meet their constraints of rhythm, rhyme, and syllable count, but these special poems are always short, so they seem doable to a young person.

Limericks, such as this example by Edward Lear, lend themselves to silly subjects that appeal to adolescents.

There was a Young Lady of Norway,
Who casually sat in a doorway;
When the door squeezed her flat,
she exclaimed, "What of that?"
This courageous young Lady of Norway.

Haiku, which requires three lines of 5, 7, and 5 syllables in that order, tends to bring out a meditative or serious side, even in young writers. The close observation that's required by haiku is wonderful practice for writers of essays, reports, and fiction. A haiku, such as my example below, is a verbal picture of one moment in time.

Dig in the wet grass,
Do not kill any small things,
Save worms for the fish.

Give middle school students many opportunities to take steps along their developmental paths by suggesting interesting writing exercises. Although even preschoolers can play some computer games, middle school students are ready to use *word processing software.*

Their fine motor skills have developed enough to learn *touch typing,* and software is available to teach children to type using games.

Ironically, when I was in high school, many teachers believed that typing skills should be taught only to those students who were likely to become secretaries! Now there is hardly a job that doesn't involve a computer, and as they turn out one written assignment after another, high school and college students are typing a lot!

I finally learned to type on my own as an adult, using vinyl records and a portable manual typewriter, but today all students can learn to type in middle school, using appropriate software for personal computers. When typing serves a useful purpose, practice seems less dull, so encourage students to type notes to relatives and friends, to send for free or inexpensive advertised items, and to submit their writing to appropriate magazines.

To publish means to place something before the public, to spread an idea about, or to make a written work well known. How can we help children become published authors? Any written work can be published in one of three ways, by *self-publishing, private publishing,* and *commercial publishing.* All three provide valuable opportunities to place children's written words before an audience.

BILLBOARD K: Three Ways to Publish

1. Self-Publishing
2. Private publishing
3. Commercial Publishing

Self-publishing is what we do every time we send a letter to someone. We place our written work in a form that can be shared with others. Every year, for example, you might send a winter holiday letter to family and friends. Copy it on your own computer, printing your letter on decorated paper, and take your holiday greetings to the post office.

Caregivers or other teachers help children self-publish every time they send home a piece of artwork, poetry, or prose. Parents help children self-publish when they send children's art to relatives who live in a different town. Invitations to birthday parties or classroom events like plays and art shows can be self-published messages. To encourage children to self-publish, parents and other teachers can demonstrate a simple technique called *yarn binding*, following ten steps.

YARN BINDING

1. Fold several papers in half, creating the book's pages. The folded edge will be bound with yarn.
2. Punch regularly spaced holes along the folded edge. Punch holes 1 inch from the edge and 1 inch apart for 5- to 7-year-olds, but smaller spaces appeal to older children.
3. Cut a piece of yarn at least four times the length of the folded edge.
4. Wrap a piece of masking tape around one end of the yarn, creating a stiffened *'needle.'*
5. Starting at the bottom edge of the book, pull the yarn through the first hole. Leave about 6 inches of yarn dangling, to secure the yarn when you're finished.
6. Pull the yarn needle in and out of the holes from bottom to top.
7. At the top of the book, loop the yarn over the top edge and back through the top hole.

8. Push the 'needle' through the next hole and loop the yarn around the side edge. Repeat.

9. Weave the yarn in this pattern down the edge of book, alternating stitches in the front and back of the book, until you reach the bottom.

10. Tie a knot or bow to secure the yarn at the bottom of the book. A yarn tassel is optional!

Older students can master this technique with little instruction. Children will soon begin to teach each other how to bind books, finding their own clever ideas to publish. Middle school students might enjoy creating treasure maps or *choose-your-own-adventure* books with multiple plots and endings.

In Julia's lower school, the teachers helped children share their writings at an *Author's Tea* where cookies and fruit punch were served. The children read their works to family members and friends, who applauded enthusiastically. Only one copy of each spiral-bound book went home, but Julia felt proud that her photocopied school picture was pasted above a line that read *About the Author*. She composed her own author's biography that included this information: *Julia used to have three pets, but now she has one—a cat named Pumpkin. She has made three books, not counting this one.*

Julia went on to publish poems and articles in commercial publications like *Stone Soup* and *Cicada*. As an adult she publishes a blog for her employer at the yarn shop, but her author's tea in lower school remains a favorite memory. If children receive early recognition for their creative efforts, they're likely to persevere.

With confidence inspired by early experience, an ambitious young person can become an entrepreneur. Julia self-published a magazine and mailed copies to her subscribers. Julia's *Goddess Magazine* was copied and stapled by a local copy shop. Forty subscribers sounds like a lot, but my financial support was required for each month's copying costs, which provided an excellent lesson in the economics of publishing.

When I was young I made carbon copies of writing that I wanted to share with family and friends. Later, mimeographed copies of my work could be made at school. When I see my articles published in magazines today, I still have the same feelings of self-affirmation that I experienced forty years ago sniffing the inky mimeographed copies fresh off the hand-cranked press. With the advent of computers and desktop publishing, producing multiple copies of children's writing became much easier.

An entire industry for self-publishing has evolved in the last few decades. Many books can help the self-publisher get started, and the magazine, *Writers' Digest*, provides many printing and publishing contacts. This magazine also co-sponsors an *International Self-Published Book Award* that might attract young authors.

The distinction between self-publishing and private publishing is subtle, but I would emphasize the identity of the publisher. When a teacher makes multiple copies of the class cookbook to send one to all the parents, I think she is acting as a private publisher.

When Julia was in kindergarten I was a private publisher, typing her classmates' stories as small books, with ample space for the children's illustrations.

As a parent I could have been considered a private publisher of Julia's *Goddess Magazine* when expenses grew, but I think I was more like an *angel* whose financing enables a theatrical troupe to produce a play. Julia herself was designing, typing, and editing the publication as a self-publisher.

As a junior, Julia was an editor of the privately published literary magazine at her high school. The school paid all expenses, but Julia and her co-editor gathered the other students' submissions, chose a fair number to publish, and edited them for clarity and consistency of format. Then the finished collection was copied commercially so enough copies would be available for teachers, students, and their relatives.

School newspapers, newsletters, cookbooks, joke books, literary magazines, and yearbooks can be examples of children's privately published written work. Both parents and teachers can become private publishers. By broadcasting children's words, adults encourage children's writing skills and invite confidence-building praise from recipients of the published product. Some very famous writers, including Walt Whitman and Virginia Woolf, published privately in the beginning of their careers.

The idea of commercial publishing can be daunting. Publishers are in a highly competitive business where profit margins are slight. Writers know that's why sending submissions to commercial publishers usually results in many more rejections than acceptances. That said, it's encouraging that a few commercial publishers regularly print children's work. Local newspapers, as one example, publish letters to the editor.

Teachers can help a class produce a dictated letter to be sent to the hometown newspaper and signed, for example, by *Mrs. Johnson's Class at Clever Neighborhood School.* Parents can encourage individual children to write about a local issue, such as an unsafe crosswalk, and send the letter to a local newspaper. This letter is likely to be published if signed by, say, Mary Prentis, age 11. Religious publications are sometimes aimed at children and might accept submissions that suit their editorial mission. Local literary magazines and some national publications will publish children's writing.

Julia published her writing nationwide, in magazines like *Stone Soup*, *Cicada*, and *Teen Voices*, as well as in regional publications like *DreamGirl*, the *Blotter*, and the *Urban Hiker*. Because the availability of such outlets frequently changes, refer to *Writer's Market* or *Merlyn's Pen* to find publications that accept submissions from children.

Students in high school can submit writings to commercial publishers, but younger children can become discouraged by repeated rejection, concluding that the world of publishing is too tough. Older children, however, might be encouraged by the intermittent reinforcement of seeing their work in a public medium like a newspaper. Such early recognition could be the start of a career! Several very famous writers, including F. Scott Fitzgerald, Benjamin Franklin, Ernest Hemingway, Langston Hughes, Stephen King, and Sylvia Plath, were first published in their teens.

BILLBOARD L: Five Reasons to Publish Children's Writing

1. To demonstrate to children that writing is a form of communication,
2. To show that writing has value in the world beyond home and school,
3. To provide validation of self-worth for children who see their words in print,
4. To give parents, grandparents, and friends a concrete product to praise, and
5. To demonstrate that all children can be authors.

Even if a child does not pursue a career in writing, there are at least five good reasons to publish children's writing, listed above in *Billboard K. First*, by publishing a child's work, a parent or teacher can demonstrate that writing is a form of communication. This realization could spur children to read, as well as to write, when they understand that articles and books will speak to them personally in the voice of an author.

Second, publishing demonstrates that writing has value in the world beyond home and school. As adults we know that good writing skills will be needed for all sorts of employment opportunities in the future. Most office workers need to compose e-mails, for example, and most supervisors need to write memos. But these kinds of activities are usually beyond children's limited experience.

Publishing, therefore, offers an early example of the value of writing in the larger world. In addition to that lesson, publishing can raise children's self-esteem by providing validation of their creativity and accomplishments. To see one's words in print can be a powerful validation of self-worth, the *third* reason to publish children's writing.

The *fourth* reason is also connected to validation. Publishing children's writing gives parents, grandparents, and neighbors a concrete product to praise and cherish.

These publications are a gift that children can give to the important adults in their lives. In this way, the children's inherent need for relatedness can be harnessed to serve the learning process.

The *fifth* reason to publish children's writing is to demonstrate that the children are already authors, just like authors whose books they love. Adults who help children see themselves as writers might attend a real book-signing someday! The author could scribble in their books, *Thank you for believing in me and encouraging my first writings.*

CHAPTER 5

In High School and Beyond

B‍Y THE TIME SHE'S A teenager, you might find your child beating you at *Scrabble* or *Blurt*. Let her gloat! In fact, offer lots of opportunities to play a variety of games involving language, such as *crossword puzzles* or *charades*. These could be healthy alternatives to turning on the television after dinner. My older daughter Linnet was pleased when we began to include her boyfriend in our *Scrabble* games, especially when he turned out to be an expert who often won the game! Linnet was proud that her parents demonstrated intellectual interest, if not excellent performance.

Older children still need encouragement to write, and often need to be inspired. They might enjoy creating artistic collages, or line drawings with written titles, rather than composing straight stories or letters. What else could inspire a high school student to write? A special spot for writing and the right tools is very encouraging. A high school student needs a writing station *(Billboard L)* equipped with different kinds of paper and pens. Plastic bins or designated drawers encourage organization of writing, drawing, painting, and collage materials. Racks for hanging files can help with the paper clutter.

A personal computer is a wonderful tool for a high school writer, but not every family can afford a computer in spite of decreasing costs. Fortunately, most schools and libraries have *computer labs* where students bring their own disks to save their work. A computer café or a copy shop is a more expensive alternative, to be used infrequently.

It's also possible to buy a good used computer at a college or university surplus store. In fact, I'm writing this book on a used computer that I purchased at the surplus store of Duke

University. I paid only about a third of the cost of my first new computer purchased over twenty years ago, which had far less capacity than my newer used machine!

Julia just purchased a portable manual typewriter on-line. Now she's interested in having her own old-fashioned printing press, the kind that was used by Benjamin Franklin and still used by specialty printers. Julia's interest in these old machines is a puzzle, because we've had a personal computer in our house since before she was born, and computers are much easier to use than printing presses! We'll encourage her fascination with early methods of publishing, however, by buying the machines we can afford.

BILLBOARD M: Writing Station Tools

different types of paper

baskets and bins for sorting

folders

ruler

protractor

stapler

scissors

hole punch

colored paper clips

envelopes of various sizes

postage stamps

address labels

markers and crayons

colored pens and pencils

cup for storing pens

glue stick

invisible tape

non-toxic glue

paints and brushes

When you're encouraging a high school writer it's sometimes necessary to be direct.

Did you write a thank you note to Grandma?
It's Aunt Sarah's 70th birthday. Would you make a card we can sign?

Maybe you can write a poem about our flood.
Is your book report finished?

Teenagers are not too old for writing classes or writing camps. Some camps are even held at prestigious colleges like Duke University. Not only can writing camps at colleges provide critiques by professors and published authors, summer camps can let young students experience life on a college campus for the first time. Such familiarity might encourage their own college attendance.

Local art centers and continuing education programs also offer writing classes that teenagers can join. Some students feel intimidated when taking classes with older adults, but a mixed age group can boost self-esteem, too. My daughter Julia had lots of attention as the youngest participant at a seminar on letterpress technique, which was held at an art center in San Francisco. Her classmates put her name at the top of the list of authors in the sample program they created.

High school students will benefit from advanced computing classes offered at their own schools, at a local community college, or at a computer camp. Familiarity with software programs for drawing, graphing, outlining, word-processing, creating data bases or web sites, can trigger healthy computer fascination in high school students.

Playwriting and performing will be attractive to some students, but others will embrace song writing, especially those who play the guitar or the piano. To encourage children to read for information, you can purchase a guide to song-writing as an unexpected present, or just buy another book on playing their chosen instrument. Reading musical notation and playing music are marvelous skills to have at any age.

High school offers the opportunity to get involved in working on a literary magazine, a school newspaper, or a yearbook. Students can submit a story, poem, drawing or article, or they can join the editorial or design staff. Not only do these extra-curricular activities provide writing experience, just holding the finished product in hand reinforces the concrete value of writing. This yearbook or playbill production will look good later, too, on college or job applications.

By the time children are in high school, they've probably developed good habits of reading and writing . . . . or maybe not. Is it too late for a parent or teacher to instill a love of reading in teenagers, or to encourage their writing skills? No, it's never too late! Some authors first books weren't published until they were in their fifties, or even in their eighties. Although Ben Franklin was already an experienced publisher and inventor in his seventies when he worked on the Declaration of Independence, that's an enormously powerful, very influential, world famous bit of writing.

At a time when teenagers are looking beyond their immediate family to firm up their personal identities, some research indicates that older children have already developed dependence on the opinions of the people who are close to them. The researchers found that most teenagers will eventually embrace the political, religious, and educational views of their parents, albeit after years of natural rebellion.

Now is the time to solidify children's good literacy habits by your example. Conspicuously read the newspapers or magazines that you enjoy. Occasionally pick up a novel instead of watching a television program, and let the family see you reading with enjoyment. Chuckle and laugh out loud as you read, and share the best parts with the people around you.

"Listen to this," I say to my husband before I read a funny paragraph out loud to him. Sometimes one of my daughters is present and notices my enjoyment of reading. Now is the time to pass on sources of information that offer objective input to teens, such as articles about health, fitness, or careers. Ideas are apt to be seriously considered by teenagers if they're expressed by an unknown author, and not by a too-familiar parent!

Gifts can be symbolic of relationships, so presents needn't be expensive to have personal meaning. A blank journal might be an inspirational gift for a young teenager who's just learning the craft of composition. And an older child will appreciate a magazine or book more than a tee shirt that doesn't match current fashion trends.

High school students appreciate magazine subscriptions that appeal to their interests in architecture, cooking, design, the environment, mechanics, music, the occult, politics, popular science, or sewing. When children are really interested in something, they're really learning! Even a silly comic book about space aliens is demonstrating writing skills, including how to plot a story, set a scene, draw characters, pace the action, deliver a message, and use metaphor and the other tools of competent writers.

Many high school students are ready to read adult chapter books and best sellers. Teens can enjoy biographies of celebrities, romance novels with sexual tension, murder mysteries or political thrillers. Talking about exciting or tragic stories with parents helps young adults feel mature and worthy of respect for their opinions.

Whether they're studying the history of the American Civil War or the Civil Rights Movement, suggest that children visit the library to check out books on their topic. Wrap up at least one book for birthdays and holidays, just to keep the importance of reading on the front burner. Some children want classic authors like Charles Dickens or Jane Austin on their bookshelves, but others want sports statistics. That's fine, as long as students are reading as an extracurricular experience, as well as for their school assignments.

Keeping a journal becomes a different experience as thought processes develop when children get older. Metacognition, or the ability to think about your own thinking, has begun to solidify for most teenagers. That's why stories, poems, and plays by college freshmen suggest self-absorption to many adult readers.

The ability to write about their own processes of feeling and thought is fairly new to older students, so teenage writing tends to be very personal. Some writers, like Sylvia Plath in *The Bell Jar*, J. D. Salinger in *The Catcher in the Rye* and Lucy Grealy in *Autobiography of a Face*, take advantage of this to appeal strongly to teenage readers.

Young adults tend to write about how they themselves are feeling at the present moment, which is developmentally appropriate at their age. However, they don't often write with attention to a reader's perspective, because young people are just realizing that they have their own unique viewpoint. To help students gain a more objective perspective, adults can encourage them to write letters to an editor about local or national issues. Brevity is a virtue in these letters, and short ones are often published. Publication can give students a real writing boost when they see their words in print, no matter how ephemeral is publication in the local newspaper's daily issue. Save this clip!

Jean Piaget, a Swiss pioneer of cognitive theory, noticed that somewhere between the ages of eleven and fifteen adolescents become able to think in abstract ways, entering what Piaget called the stage of *Formal Operational Thought*, or higher level thinking. Other theorists of development realized that logical thinking was not an automatic gift of age, but required schooling, or some other kind of specific training.

The ability to think abstractly is what allows high school students to understand the rules of *formal grammar*. Because the subject of grammar is very abstract, introducing it too early discourages many young students from pursuing writing. An awareness of grammar can make writing sound too difficult to younger children, but older students actually can enjoy the study of grammar because it presents an abstract puzzle to be solved.

A young high school student can be introduced to the parts of speech, such as the *subject* and *predicate* of a sentence, and the *nouns, pronouns, verbs, adjectives, adverbs* and *prepositions*. An older high school student can use the famous *Elements of Style* by Strunk and White, a compact guide to grammar and word usage, which is available in several paperback editions. This readable little book explains details like the difference between *imply* and *infer*, and what is meant by a *split infinitive*.

A thick dictionary like *Merriam-Webster's Collegiate Dictionary* also makes a great present for a student in high school. Appendices with abbreviations, brief biographical and geographic entries, foreign words and phrases, a guide to grammar and style, a list of colleges, and even a few pictures make a good dictionary a necessary tool for any writer.

Adults who enjoy reading about grammar and word derivation can chuckle over *The King's English: A Guide to Modern Usage* by Kingsley Amis. Reference books deserve a whole shelf in a student's home office. You'll find suggestions for writing resources in *Appendix VII, Guides to Grammar and Editing for Writers*. Although a precocious high school junior or senior might use such resources, college students will benefit more from sophisticated, abstract information about the English language.

Teenagers might be ready to read about the art of writing. Guides to writing for older children are listed in *Appendix V, Literary Resources for Adults*. Students can feel important, like real authors, when they have a subscription to a magazine about writing. Enter *writers magazines* on your search engine to locate these excellent publications.

POETS AND WRITERS MAGAZINE
Poets & Writers, Inc.
212-226-3586 www.pw.org

THE WRITER
Kalmbach Publishing Co.

1-800-558-1544, ext. 818

www.writermag.com

WRITER'S DIGEST

F+W Media, Inc.

513-531-2690 www.writersdigest.com

TEEN INK

1-800-363-1986

www.teeninc.com

Children need to see examples of parents' writing, like shopping lists, lists of chores, lists of gifts they'd like for a birthday, Mother's Day, or Channukuh, and thank-you notes.

Thank you for taking out the garbage Sue!
Nice to come home to a cleaner kitchen.
Love, Dad

The lawn looks great, Bill. You finished the mowing
when your favorite TV program was on!
From your grateful Mom

Designate one drawer or cardboard box where samples of children's writings will be saved, including clips of letters-to-the-editor, book reports, Valentine's Day cards, and shopping lists. The whole family will be amused when you look at these later, or when your children have their own children. Encourage timely submissions to appropriate contests and magazines. By the time Julia was sixteen she had a resume with almost thirty publications! She won a writing contest at our local public library, an honorable mention in a literary magazine, and second place for a poem sent to a contest.

When a high school student is a junior or senior, it's time to apply for college. A few publications or awards in writing contests will demonstrate that this is a serious student. But beyond admission, a number of college tuition scholarships depend on *essay writing*. Purchase a guide to scholarships and encourage all possible applications. Even if a student doesn't win or place in a contest, the experience of composing a required essay will strengthen children's writing skills.

Students in high school can be on their way to becoming great writers, but maintaining motivation is necessary for continuing to improve composition skills. Most parents and other teachers make small mistakes as they try to support young writers. The letters A, B, C, D in *Billboard M* can be a mnemonic device to help you avoid mistakes.

BILLBOARD N: Maintaining Student Motivation for Writing

1. **A**void Arrogance
2. **B**e Bendable, not Brittle
3. **C**ancel the Critic
4. **D**on't Demand writing

First, AVOID ARROGANCE. Don't suggest that you're more knowledgeable than a young person. People become discouraged if they feel incapable of an achievement. Children can abandon writing if they believe they lack ability or knowledge. Many adults dislike mathematics because, as a school subject, math was taught to them in a top-down fashion, making it seem too difficult. Children tend to be very open to humble adults, but distrustful of the arrogant ones, so avoid bossy phrases like these.

> *Here, let me show you how . . .*
> *No, that's not the right way . . .*
> *No, I think you're wrong . . .*

Instead of sounding arrogant, try to sound interested. Have humility when helping children write. You could be nurturing the next Agatha Christie, Roald Dahl, Michael Crichton, Steven King, J. K. Rowling, or William Shakespeare, so always be supportive.

> *Fascinating! (Exciting, clever, informative, thoughtful)*
> *That works! Tell me more about your idea.*
> *What else could you say in this situation?*
> *Do you want a little feedback on that?*

Second, BE BENDABLE, NOT BRITTLE. Don't be disappointed when a child conceives a writing project like a poem or story, only to abandon it in an embryonic state. If you are disappointed, try not to let the young writer know about your feelings. Any writing, no matter how minimal, serves as practice for later writing.

I started my first novel in elementary school and it still haunts me. In that attempt at age nine, I didn't know that I was grappling with a theme I wouldn't wrestle to the ground until I was over fifty! But my struggle with a few pages of the story made me believe I could come up with a theme that was worthy of a novel. That experience helped me believe I could be a writer, although my thin spiral stenographer's pad was never filled.

Both my daughters have unfinished writing projects that thrilled and tickled me when I first heard about them. Why couldn't the girls keep writing, I lamented. Didn't Linnet's novel *Wisteria Mansion* have the seeds of a great mystery? Why isn't Julia working on her book about music criticism?

Don't press your children the way I did, because as far as those specific projects were concerned, I had no positive effect. Just as playing with building blocks is good practice for a developing architect, playing with words is great practice for future authors. No matter if the product is almost entirely in the mind of the child, just a temporary idea as wispy as a cloud, thinking about writing counts as practice in composition. Remember that a creative breeze could be blowing through, so try to bend in the wind!

Third, CANCEL THE CRITIC. Criticism can have unintended but extremely long-lasting effects. Let me share a sad story about some well-meant but misguided criticism I received in my own childhood. Christmas was celebrated in our public school with enthusiasm. Teetering on noisy wooden bleachers, we kindergartners, whatever our family's religious faith, sang Christmas carols for our parents. Dressed as angels, we wore costumes made of white bed sheets cut on the bias to create wide sleeves for wings, and our halos were made of bent silver pipe cleaners.

The pageant could have been lovely, but I still remember that day with sadness, because our Christmas art project overshadowed the performance. We were making Christmas cards for our mothers. The cards would be hung high on a clothesline, strung across the front of the kindergarten classroom. I was intrigued by all the colorful art materials and I wanted to sprinkle some glitter, which would be a new experience. Immediately I bent my head over my project, straight hair brushing the green construction paper. I quickly decorated my card with lots of red crayoned balls. Ornaments made my drawing look like a real Christmas tree! Just like the tree we had in our living room at home . . .

Suddenly my teacher snatched the tree from under my hand and held it over my head. "This," she said, "is the wrong way to make your card." My kindergarten teacher announced to the whole class that I hadn't waited for the full instructions, and now my Christmas tree would never be right! The glitter couldn't be added *after* the crayon because it couldn't stick to it. She hoped no one else was making the same mistake.

I was devastated, and not only because I'd been scolded. I had ruined my mother's card, so she would be the only mother who didn't get a beautiful Christmas card. It was my own fault. I hadn't waited for directions, and now I'd hurt my mother. The weight of guilt was hardly bearable as I dragged myself home, not able to play my usual sidewalk games. That's how I learned that adults must be careful about criticizing children!

More than fifty-five years later I can still feel my shame in that kindergarten classroom, but more significant was my chronic lack of pleasure in creating visual art after that painful experience. In elementary school, in high school, in college, and in graduate school I frequently had to draw or paint or sculpt in class, but I didn't enjoy those activities and would never consider myself a *visual artist*. I'm very lucky that no one told me my writing was somehow wrong or hurtful, so I kept writing all my life. Thank goodness my writing skills weren't killed by thoughtless criticism!

Adults in writing groups often learn that avoiding negative criticism is one of the group's main rules. As an adult I became tearful when a member of my writing group criticized my work as *overly expository* and *lacking action*. I found myself blubbering in front of other grown-ups, so I couldn't share any more of my writing with them. Criticism can be a creativity killer, so it's better to point to what is good in a student writing sample. Be constructive, but not critical!

> *I love your adjectives! They make me feel like I'm right there.*
> *The section where you talk about your dog's antics is really funny.*
> *What exciting action! Give me more examples of action.*
> *I can feel that boy's anticipation before the big event.*

Fourth, DON'T DEMAND that children write if, at just that moment, they're really not interested in writing. When we demand that children practice writing, we put composition in the same category as homework. Grownups can tell children their homework is a very valuable activity, but children suspect that most homework is merely busywork.

CHAPTER 6

Maintaining Motivation

Higher education helped me raise the excellent writers that my daughters have become. Information about children's motivation contributed to my experience as a parent and teacher. Insights from educational research can help you support young writers, too.

We human beings are very inquisitive creatures. Evolution equipped us with innate curiosity, which is an powerful tool for adaptation to our environment. Curiosity, the basis of most learning, contributed to our survival as a species.

Whenever human beings discovered the cause of some phenomenon, they could begin to control it. For example, our curious ancestors who learned why a fire will spread, that a fire will burn out without fuel, and how fire can be moved and used for warmth and cooking, gained an enormous advantage over other animals in life's ongoing struggle.

When our ancestors began to ask themselves why different animals behave in certain ways, they gained a real advantage over nature. Understanding the *why* of behavior gave human beings the power of prediction! They could now predict the movements of animals, which enabled them to hunt more efficiently. When they learned to predict the behavior of other people, they could become effective leaders, able to control other human beings. Using this evolutionary advantage, human parents still observe their children's actions and ask themselves, *why do they do that?*

Being able to understand children's motivation gives parents and other teachers three important advantages *(Billboard M)*. *First,* when we understand why children do what they do, it's easier to get them to do what we *want* them to do. With insight from the field of child development, we can consciously motivate children to behave in ways we think are useful and appropriate.

When we insist that a green vegetable be eaten before the ice cream is served, we're using our understanding of children's motivation to achieve a short-term goal. A *second* advantage gained by understanding children's motivation is the ability to achieve an important long-term goal that most parents share. Many of us have a goal of raising self-regulated, self-directed communicators. We know that people who communicate well, both orally and in writing, can experience more success in life.

A *third* advantage to understanding motivation has to do with a greater enjoyment of our children. When we understand children better, we begin to see certain behaviors in a more positive light, behaviors that are evidence of children's learning and maturation. When we recognize developmental progress clearly, we delight in children's achievements.

BILLBOARD O: Three Reasons to Learn about Motivation

1. To get children to do what we want them to do,
2. To raise self-regulated, self-directed communicators, and
3. To enjoy our children more.

My introduction to the importance of motivation in children's learning came during one of my first experiences as a teacher. When I was an undergraduate student in education at the State University of New York at New Paltz, I spent time as a *Participant* in a classroom at the campus lab school.

I was very fortunate to be placed in the *Open Primary Classroom*, which was loosely based on the *British Infant School* model. This program was staffed by two head teachers, two assistant teachers, two student teachers, and two participants. Serving approximately fifty-five students in first through third grade, the classroom occupied the space traditionally used by three self-contained classes. What great training for dealing with any occasionally chaotic classroom!

Near the end of every school day in the *Open Primary Classroom*, time was reserved for teachers to read to their young students. During the afternoon class meeting, each adult gave a brief pitch for the book she would be reading that day. Because these teachers supported student autonomy, they allowed all children to listen to a book of their choice from among several books to be read aloud. Furthermore, if children preferred to read a book on their own, they were not required to listen to a read-aloud.

Teachers, student teachers, participants and volunteers read to the children from a wide variety of literary materials. Some adults could be reading from chapter books, while others might read a short story or a fable. In one afternoon a nonfiction selection on science that described the job of an astronaut, a history text about schooling in colonial times, and a book of nonsense poems could be offered.

Most children made their choices quickly, and they stayed with one teacher's reading group until their chapter book was finished, or until the teacher chose a different theme like animal stories. Not surprisingly, friends often encouraged children to choose a particular reading group. There they sat in a friendly bunch listening to a book, leaning against each other at the teacher's feet.

Unfortunately, a few children never sat through a whole story or a whole chapter. A few students spent the reading period wandering from one group to another, never demonstrating sustained interest. The teachers speculated about these children. Could they have attention problems, unusually high activity levels, or auditory processing problems? Did they lack parental modeling, or lack experience with books?

Patiently the teachers invited them to listen to one selection after another, but day after day the small group of wanderers moved restlessly from room to room. Because these teachers respected children's autonomy, they never forced them to stay for a whole selection, as long as the children were not disruptive.

One day I was approached by a third grader who asked me to read his book aloud. Maybe he wisely asked *me* because I was the youngest and newest *Participant* in the classroom. Wanting acceptance from the children, I quickly agreed. Suddenly a cluster of small boys surrounded me, which was gratifying, but when I saw the book, my heart sank. This book seemed as unsuitable and dull for children as the congressional record!

This book was not a story at all, but an encyclopedic list of sports statistics with small photographs of athletes. An athlete's batting average, or the number of passes he'd intercepted, were printed under a small photo. No actual paragraphs in this book! Instead of a read-aloud, it was more like an almanac with answers to trivia questions.

Gamely I opened the book and began to read meaningless words and numbers, trying to infuse them with as much varied inflection and enthusiasm as I could muster. I grinned and frowned. I raised and lowered my eyebrows. I gestured with my free hand, suggesting enormous significance by spreading my fingers and flinging my arm at the ceiling. I made eye contact with each member of my audience.

Then I realized that sports statistics held the full attention of these children! They were all listening to me, completely involved in the reading experience. No child deserted my reading group, and more children joined us until our group contained all the boys who'd been labeled hyperactive or inattentive. Our allotted reading time was over before their attention flagged.

"Are you gonna read from that book tomorrow?" a boy asked. "Sure," I said. "It's a great book!" Yes, a *great* book, although I couldn't understand one phrase. I read from that great thick book again and again, and always had an audience hanging on every word. That sports encyclopedia was a real learning experience for me. In my naive willingness to take a detour from educationally appropriate books, I learned four significant facts about children's motivation.

BILLBOARD P: Four Facts about Motivation

1. Motivation for learning resides in each child,
2. Children's intrinsic motivation can be tapped to enhance learning,
3. Children's interests can be an indicator of their intrinsic motivation, and
4. By following children's interests, adults facilitate children's learning.

Almost twenty years after that real-life demonstration of the power of children's interests, I wrote my doctoral dissertation on *teachers' beliefs about interest and learning*. As early as 1744, pioneering educator John Newbery had connected children's games like 'base-ball' to moral lessons. In Newbery's picture book, *A Little Pretty Pocket-Book, Intended for the Instruction and Amusement of Little Master Tommy and Pretty Miss Polly*, he linked children's entertainment like sports and games to their motivation for learning.

Motivation is a psychological construct, a conventional way to refer to a phenomenon that has no measurable physical existence, but can be recognized by its effect on people. Another psychological construct is the notion of *love*. We can't measure love with a thermometer or a ruler, but we notice its effects on human behavior. One measure of a husband's love, for example, could be the number of televised sports events he misses to attend Sunday dinner at his mother-in-law's house. We recognize motivation when we see such effects on behavior, but motivation is nothing physical to be held in our hands.

Stated as a formal definition from the field of educational psychology, motivation is *an underlying force or stimulus that impels a person to act in a certain way*. To motivate someone is to move that person to take action. Other synonyms or concepts closely related to motivation include *incentive, drive, impulse, influence,* and *inducement*. When we ask ourselves, "Why do children do that?" we are asking, "What motivates children?"

The study of motivation examines the *why of learning*. Why do people learn to do some things more easily than others? Throughout the 20th century, theorists of motivation like Dewey, Thorndike, White, Erikson, Maslow, Piaget, deCharms, Deci and Ryan, wrote about why children behave in specific ways. Parents and other teachers are interested in children's motivation to behave in typically childish ways, and how adults can motivate children to behave in ways that will be valuable when their children are grown.

An understanding of human motivation relies on our knowledge of the *unconscious*. The unconscious mind is not easily accessed in conscious thought, but reveals itself through dreams and unintended actions. Mental processes are always taking place on an unconscious level, where our minds are very active. Many therapists try to reveal people's unconscious thoughts to change their unhealthy behaviors.

Sigmund Freud emphasized the power of the unconscious in 19th century Vienna and London. Freud discovered that some of his patients' apparently physical illnesses were actually *psychological*, or caused by unconscious thoughts. This insight led Freud to try psychological treatment for his patients' physical problems. Today such therapy is known to be one effective solution for psychological problems, and is used by many counselors and therapists to improve patients' lives.

Sometimes I catch a glimpse of the unconscious processes in my own life. One day I misread the phrase a *censored* account as an *endorsed* account. Because that reading made no sense in context, I glanced at the words again and easily read the phrase correctly. What an odd mistake to make! If I read from left to right as I scan a line, it's hard to understand how I scrambled and substituted certain letters. How, especially, did I get the first letter of the word wrong?

Research demonstrates that when we read text, our eyes don't move only from left to right, from one letter to the next. Reading is more than translating written symbols into sounds, and then recalling the meaning of those sounds. Mature reading is more than simple phonics, although reading skills might be built upon phonics at first. Readers actually use many complex mental processes to read.

How did I mistake *censored* for *endorsed*? Instead of merely scanning letter by letter from left to right, a part of my mind was searching my memory for matches to each cluster of letters that resembled a word. When I misread the word *censored*, part of my brain was unconsciously skipping ahead of my eyes. Much more was happening in my mind than simple decoding, using only skills of phonics.

The word *account* had already been unconsciously recognized by one part of my mind. Then another part recognized many of the letters in the previous word, *censored*. My mind tried to attach meaning to what I was reading. I knew the word *account* had several possible definitions, as in a *checking account* or a *newspaper account* of a burglary. In a split second, my unconscious mind chose the banking-related meaning of the word.

Did that happen because a few letters (e, n, s, o, r, e, d) could be scrambled to become the banking-related word *endorse*? Or did the choice of a banking-related meaning of *account* influence the misreading of *censored* because I was unconsciously expecting another banking-related word? Was the search for meaning affected by being seated at the same desk where I pay bills? Or was the misreading influenced by a low level of anxiety about my financial situation, which makes banking-related words important to me? I can speculate, but I can't be sure. Maybe a combination of influences caused the mistake.

When we're reading, we're almost always unaware of the speedy and complicated mental processes that are occurring. An interesting mistake can remind us that our brains are always incredibly busy, performing multiple simultaneous tasks unavailable to our consciousness. Humor, for example, always relies on subconscious levels of thought.

Have you heard the joke about the man who, mishearing *brain* as *train,* asked St. Peter for a short one? The humor inherent in a Freudian slip relies on our knowledge of the unconscious layers of thought that influence speech. Motivation also takes place at an unconscious level. Adults might be unaware of what motivates children to behave in specific ways, but they can make an educated guess based on accepted theory. For example, the teacher who attributes a preschooler's regressive thumb-sucking to the arrival of a new baby in the family is relying on belief based on Freudian theory.

Attributing human behavior to specific motivation requires that an observer accept specific theory. Behavioral scientists who came after Freud, including John B. Watson and B. F. Skinner in the 20th century, stayed away from explanations of behavior that relied on invisible mental activity. Watson and Skinner preferred to explain behavior by what they could observe, such as the presence of reinforcement or punishment that increased or decreased behaviors.

A caregiver who hands out colorful stickers to reward a preschooler for using the toilet bases that practice on a behaviorist theory of motivation. They usually call this activity toilet *training* instead of toilet *teaching*, which hints at behavioristic methods. Most parents and other teachers want to foster *more versus less* motivation, but all children have differing types and amounts of motivation.

Richard M. Ryan and Edward L. Deci refined previous theories that dealt with the types of motivation. Deci and Ryan focused on the distinction between *intrinsic* and *extrinsic* motivators, such as these sources of motivation for writers, listed below in *Billboard P*.

BILLBOARD Q: Intrinsic and Extrinsic Motivation

EXTRINSIC MOTIVATORS
Tangible reinforcement for writing like treats,
Praise for writing skill from parents and teachers,
Grades earned for good writing, and
Money or scholarships earned from publication.

INTRINSIC MOTIVATORS
Interest in topics or processes of writing,
Pride in self-expression,

Satisfaction in communication,
Satisfaction in writing skills, and
Pride in publication.

Extrinsic motivation is caused by something external or *outside* the individual. A young child can be extrinsically motivated to sort attribute blocks by the promise of a sticker from her occupational therapist. Adults are usually extrinsically motivated to hold jobs so they receive paychecks.

The source of *intrinsic* motivation is internal, or *within* the individual. A six-year-old could be intrinsically motivated by his pride in accomplishment to practice his handwriting carefully. I'm intrinsically motivated to write about early childhood development and early education because I want to help children grow in healthy ways. My satisfaction continues to be my intrinsic motivator, because educational publications are rarely lucrative.

This distinction, however, does not imply that extrinsically motivated behaviors cannot be self-chosen, or that extrinsic motivation is less valuable than intrinsic motivation. Extrinsic and intrinsic motivations always interact, and tend to support each other. People are motivated both intrinsically and extrinsically, depending on their locus of control.

Locus of control, another psychological construct, refers to whether we feel we're in charge of ourselves, or feel like some external person or force is controlling us. Most people want to feel they themselves are in charge. That's why the thought of prison, where we would lose all control of when and where we eat, whom we see, and what we do all day, is really frightening to most of us.

To explore your own feelings about being in control, you can take the following short *Locus of Control Self-Assessment*. This exercise can be interpreted as your perception of personal control. Of these fifteen statements, how many indicate that *external* factors affect you? How many indicate that *internal* factors affect you? Do your scores surprise you? How does your more internal or external locus of control affect your life?

A LOCUS OF CONTROL SELF-ASSESSMENT

Carefully read each statement below. Mark all statements *True* or *False* (T or F) based only on your personal beliefs. There are no right or wrong answers. These statements are designed to make you think about your locus of control. After indicating your personal beliefs, mark the statements that indicate an *Internal* or *External* locus of control (I or E) on the lines to the right. Please don't leave any statements unmarked, no matter how unsure you feel about your answers!

T/F   I/E

___ Getting a raise is due to hard work.   ___

___ Getting a good grade in a course is due to my effort.   ___

___ It is not important to vote in elections.   ___

___ I earn all the honors and recognition I receive.   ___

___ A person can get rich by gambling and winning.   ___

___ I need to remain informed about the world.   ___

___ Sometimes I don't know who my real friends are.   ___

___ I often can convince friends that I am right.   ___

___ The raises I get are due to my boss's moods.   ___

___ The jobs I get are a matter of whom I know.   ___

___ The children I work with make me lose my temper.   ___

___ You have to be in the right place at the right time.   ___

___ I can change the future of a child.   ___

___ Your success depends on where you were born.   ___

___ The right education can make you successful.   ___

TOTALS   True ____ False ____
                       Internal ____ External ____

Because adults often want to feel they're in control, it can be hard for them to let children be in charge. But all children, especially toddlers, need their *autonomy*. Teaching will go more smoothly if we remember that children often have an *internal locus of control*. Adults can harness children's intrinsic motivation by offering a choice of learning activities Choices will help children learn more effectively!

Intrinsic motivation arises from our basic human needs that developed over a long evolutionary history. Our innate need for relatedness, for example, is the tendency of human beings to seek connections with other people. Such connections can be very valuable throughout development. The healthy need for mastery or competence drives children to accomplish goals, and the normal need for autonomy pushes them to achieve goals on their own. "Me do!" says a toddler.

According to theorists like Deci and Ryan, the psychological needs for *mastery, autonomy,* and *relatedness*, three primary motivational forces, may be our most basic psychological energizers of behavior. From birth a human being is an active agent exercising capacities and interests, the evidence of a developing self. This *self* is the source of our intrinsically motivated behaviors, those behaviors growing out of our innate psychological needs.

CHAPTER 7

Encouraging Interests

WHAT TOPICS INTEREST CHILDREN? PARENTS and teachers need to know the answer to this question because studies demonstrate that an interested child is a child who is learning! In fact, educational researchers tell us that the higher the child's interest level, the better the learning. This could seem counter-intuitive if you believe that learning is supposed to be hard, but for most children, learning is actually fun!

Studies of young children's interests are sometimes limited by preschoolers' developing ability to *self-report*. That's why my research used teachers' perceptions as a window into the observable interests of young children. Some parents and teachers believe that children develop strong interests only after the early years. However, anecdotal evidence and research both indicate that children often enter their first preschool classroom with some well-focused interests. How can parents and other teachers learn about children's interests, and how their interests will affect learning?

Interest is another invisible psychological construct. A definition from the field of Educational Psychology states that interest includes a child's stored knowledge about a particular object, topic, or activity, and the child's value for that object. Teachers know children's interests often influence them to behave in ways that promote learning. The interested child is aroused or excited, wants to become involved in activities and materials, and maintains involvement over time. This behavior will lead to learning.

For older children, researchers found that the most powerful learning occurs when students' prior knowledge and interests have been well matched to instructional activities. A number of studies found that when interest is present, children's learning may be more efficient, because interest provides the characteristics in *Billboard R*.

BILLBOARD R: What Children's Interest Provides

1. Faster orientation to topics and materials,
2. Increased attention,
3. Higher comprehension,
4. Better use of learning strategies,
5. Better memory, and
6. More positive emotions about learning.

Educational researchers distinguish between two types of interest, *situational* and *individual interest*. This distinction is useful to parents and other teachers who are committed to *developmentally appropriate practice* (DAP). These adults recognize that all children pass through similar developmental stages, but do so in ways unique to each individual child.

Specific features of the environment can evoke situational interest. Situational interest tends to affect children of similar age and background in a similar way. Five-year-old boys from contemporary middle class American homes might be interested in television superheroes. Around my home in North Carolina, boys tend to be interested in race cars!

Individual interest, on the other hand, comes out of a personal history and varies greatly from child to child. A boy whose mother works for an airline might develop a strong interest in planes. A girl whose father races cars might have interests in identifying automobiles and in mechanics.

In 1913, educational philosopher John Dewey emphasized the importance of children's interests. He accused teachers of two common errors. Teachers made mistakes when they selected subject matter regardless of children's interests, and when they used clever methods to dress up otherwise meaningless material. Dewey directed teachers to figure out how previously existing characteristics or behaviors of children could be used to teach new skills or information, stressing the importance of children's innate interests.

In 1935, in contrast to Dewey, educational psychologist E. L. Thorndike stated that children's interests are learned over time and are entirely dependent upon experience, rather than being innate. Thorndike suggested that the task of educators was to form appropriate new appropriate interests in children.

Parents and other teachers can follow the practical advice of both Dewey and Thorndike to enhance children's learning. First they can uncover children's established interests, capitalizing on both situational and individual interests. Second, they can present topics that are less intrinsically interesting to children, like dental health, in ways that will pique their interest. Compared to teachers of older children, parents and teachers of young children have a lot of freedom to design learning activities for children.

Because an emergent curriculum is only an ideal that many teachers strive for, some teachers still organize their curriculum around units, themes, or topics. Themes can guide their choice of daily learning activities. My sample unit plan for introducing the alphabet letters P and W, for example, could spark children's interest in manuscript writing. A preschool teacher could plan a unit on *Apples* for two weeks in September, and a unit on the *Circus* for three weeks in the spring. With experience, teachers can use children's interests to guide their choice of classroom activities.

Taking advantage of typical characteristics of early childhood programs, my research used teachers' perception of children's interest in classroom topics to reflect children's actual interests. Teachers of young children, in contrast to teachers of older students, have smaller class sizes, greater opportunity for one-on-one and small-group interaction. They tend to provide learning experiences, rather than lectures or teacher-directed activities.

Those developmentally appropriate classroom characteristics enable early childhood teachers of 3- to 7-year-olds to observe children's varying interests, particularly those situational interests shared by many children. A random sample of over 200 generous teachers responded to my mailed survey. They resided in 46 states and taught in urban, suburban and rural communities at various socioeconomic levels, in both public and private schools. They taught large and small classes of typically developing children, as well as children with special educational needs.

The responding teachers' educational preparation ranged from on-the-job training to multiple advanced degrees. In short, they formed a representative sample of early childhood teachers nationwide, so they provided important information about the interests of the children in their classes. This information may be useful to parents and other teachers who want to capitalize on children's intrinsic motivation for learning.

A questionnaire on children's interest in classroom topics required open-ended responses from teachers. To avoid influencing the teachers' perceptions, no list of sample topics was provided. Responding teachers generated three topics taught in the previous year that were the most and least interesting to the children in their classrooms. Some teachers offered their observations and advice based on their classroom experience.

TEACHERS TALK ABOUT CHILDREN'S INTERESTS

1. My coworkers and I have worked hard to develop an emergent curriculum in our classroom this year, as well as webbing in our planning sessions. This has made all the difference in our classroom dynamics and interests.

2. We have been working together to really listen to the children, to get ideas about what interests them. *Outer Space* lasted close to two months!

3. The children did a lot of extensions on their own with themes like *Native American, African,* and *Mexican Cultures; Dinosaurs, Geography,* and *Space.*

4. Most written curricula limit the teachers and are all too detailed. Children love things that are familiar, and children love to laugh!

5. Any interest or theme that has lots of hands-on and active participation, and that starts with familiar props, experiences, and ideas, will engage children.

6. The children are much more interested in a theme when they are involved. In our spring garden the children plant seeds, watch caterpillars and tadpoles change, and collect bugs and seeds. We live at the shore three blocks from the ocean, so the sea interests our children.

Teachers also listed up to three topics that they did not teach, but were of high interest to children. These teachers provided almost 1800 individual responses! When these responses were compiled, they identified more than 115 high- and low-interest topics.

The 1800 topics were condensed into 30 topic categories. The topic *Famous People,* for example, was listed by only one teacher as being of interest to children, so it was placed under *Social Studies.* The 30 categories were ranked according to how often teachers listed them as being of high or low interest. The results of this study duplicated findings from my pilot study conducted two years earlier, strengthening these new findings.

What topics are most interesting to young children? Children's single most frequently identified interest is in *Animals*. Including specific topics like *Monkeys*, the responding teachers identified *Animals* 274 times as a classroom topic of high interest. Confirming this result, animals of various types were listed as a topic of low interest only 20 times.

Because they are extinct, *Dinosaurs* were not grouped under the general category of *Animals*, but more than half the teachers in the study (114) indicated that *Dinosaurs* was a topic of very high interest to the children in their class. *Dinosaurs* was listed almost as frequently by teachers of all young children from the age of 3 to 7.

Fantasy, a category that included topics like *fairy tales, nursery rhymes, castles, monsters,* and *the circus*, was a high-interest topic in 60 classrooms, but listed as low interest in 15 classrooms. *Space* or *Astronomy*, in contrast, had a high-interest frequency of 53, but was listed only 9 times as a low-interest topic, giving it a similar high rating.

Topics like *magnets, gravity, machines,* and *light* were grouped under the category of *Science*. With an overall frequency of 54, science topics in general were of high interest to children. *Geology*, the most popular subcategory under *Science*, includes *rocks, minerals* and *volcanoes*. *Plants*, including *gardening, seeds,* and *trees*, was listed as a high-interest topic 38 times. The topic *Plants*, however, could be included under the general category of *Science*, raising that frequency to 92. Small plants and rocks are concrete objects to be touched or held, making them popular with children.

At the other end of the scale, the general category of *Academics* was the topic listed most frequently (67) as being of low interest to young children. Under this umbrella term were topics like *colors, shapes, letters, numbers, money, calendar, time, patterning, ordering,* and *math*. *Health/nutrition/safety* (44) and *seasons/weather* (40) were the next least interesting topics in early childhood classrooms.

It's alarming that topics under the category of *Academics* were listed so often as being of low interest to children! This research suggests that some teachers have a didactic approach to academics. Rather than integrating abstract academic skills like *patterning* and *letter recognition* into the context of theme-based units, some teachers are focusing on abstract concepts in relative isolation.

Parents and other teachers can use my research findings to improve children's academic progress. By referring to the *interest index* and *topic frequency ratings* below, they can evaluate their teaching. Classroom teachers can study last year's lesson plans, looking for unit topics that have a high-interest rating, and parents can provide high interest books and activities at home. Then they can address academic concepts through topical units that interest many children. Creative teachers can expand their repertoire of activities, using this list of topics to generate fresh ideas.

Harnessing a less interesting topic to a more interesting one is a valuable teaching technique! *The Four Seasons,* for example, is a frequently taught *low-interest* topic in early childhood classrooms. But armed with a list of children's situational interests, teachers can incorporate information about seasonal change within a unit on *Butterflies* or *Bears,* capitalizing on the children's typical interest in animals.

Concepts like *color, size, shape, letter recognition,* and *time* could be taught through fantasy or animal themes. In this way children can slowly develop interests in the abstract topics that are stressed within traditional academics. When they study *telling time,* children can move the hands on a clock face as *Goldilocks and the Three Bears* move through their day. Using a flannel board, children can arrange items in the bears' house by size. *The Three Little Pigs* can be used to introduce ordinal numbers. *Caps for Sale: A Tale of a Peddler, Some Monkeys and Their Monkey Business* by Esphyr Slobodkina considers color names, cause and effect, and temporal sequence.

Parents and other teachers can conduct their own research about the situational and individual interests of the children in their care. Classroom teachers can make informal observations of children's self-chosen activities, or teachers can direct children to vote for their preferred topics.

In a more elaborate strategy, teachers will administer interest inventories to children and their families. The results of their investigations can influence the range of activities offered in their classrooms. After noting topics that appeal to girls, or appeal mainly to boys, a teacher can offer a more gender-balanced curriculum, encouraging both boys and girls to cross boundaries of gender stereotypes by trying a wide variety of activities.

For children at risk for low school achievement or motivational problems, accurate information on children's interests can be used to design educational interventions. The adults who capitalize on children's interests make learning activities more inviting, enhancing both the emotional climate for children, and how much they learn.

TEACHERS' INTEREST INVENTORY FOR CHILDREN

1. I'm going to read many books out loud in school this year. What kinds of books do you want me to read? What should the books be about?

2. If a sitter asks you to pick out a video to watch before bedtime, what do you want the video to be about?

3. If a genie told you that you could go anywhere you wanted, to look at anything at all, what would you want to see?

4. What is the most interesting topic to talk about? Some children are interested in *trains, horses, soccer, cooking,* or *trees.* What are you most interested in?

5. What are you curious about? What topic do you want to learn more about?

TEACHERS' INTEREST INVENTORY FOR FAMILIES

Please name three topics that interest your child, as well as three topics that don't interest the child in my class.

MOST interesting: LEAST interesting:

1._____   1._____
2._____   2._____
3._____   3._____

CHILDREN'S INTEREST INDEX AND TOPIC FREQUENCY RATINGS

Topic Taught	Interest Level	Number Reports
Animals (all)	Very High	274
Insects	Very High	50
Ocean	Very High	40
Pets	Very High	38
Farm	High	24
Reptiles	Moderate	16
Zoo	Moderate	13
Dinosaurs	Very High	114
Fantasy (all)	Very High	60
Fantasy in Books	Moderate	18
Outer Space	Very High	53
Science (all)	High	54
Rocks	Moderate	15
Plants	High	38
Multicultural	High	35
Native American	Moderate	16
Academics (all)	Very Low	35
Mathematics	Very Low	9
Transportation	High	31
Cooking	High	29
Super Heroes	High	28
Sports	High	26
Social Studies	Low	25
Drama	High	23
Holidays	Moderate	23
Occupations	Moderate	20

CHAPTER 8

Exercises to Build Young Writers

LIKE ANY MUSCLES, THE WRITING muscles are built slowly, and they take proper nutrition and exercise to build. Of course, this is just a figure of speech, but writing does use the brain, and brains do control muscles, which must be exercised to maintain health and strength. The ability to write well is a learned skill, like cooking delicious meals or playing a musical instrument. No one is born with high level skills. Even very talented bakers or musicians will expend a lot of time and effort working to reach their full potential.

Building a writer requires the healthy nutrition provided by books, magazines, and other reading materials, as well as interesting writing exercises designed for each age group. Use my writing exercises in this chapter, design your own exercises, or see other books about teaching writing, such as those listed in *Appendix V, Literacy Resources for Adults*. Parents and other teachers will find workbooks containing more writing exercises at their local bookstores, at discount stores, or even at their grocery store.

BILLBOARD S: Four Reasons to Use Writing Exercises

1. To promote fine motor control and representation in kindergarten,
2. To teach the mechanics of writing in primary school,
3. To maintain writing motivation in middle school, and
4. To stimulate writing composition in high school.

KINDERGARTEN WRITING EXERCISES

1. FAVORITE PEOPLE

Ask the children to list their favorite people. Take dictation from children to fill blanks on prepared papers. For each person named, children finish these sentences:

I like _____ *because* _____ .
I want to <u>*(do something or go somewhere)*</u> *with* _____ .

The completed sentences can be glued to drawing paper so children can draw a picture for each sentence. These make wonderful bulletin boards with captions that can be '*read*' by the children themselves.

2. TIC-TAC-TOE

Teach children to play Tic-Tac-Toe. Create four simple game boards for each child by drawing two vertical lines crossed by two horizontal lines. Keep a number of game boards on hand so this educational game can be pulled out whenever time allows.

Explain that two children play on one board. The children take turns printing either an O or an X in their chosen square. The goal of the game is to place three of the same symbols in a line. Symbols can line up horizontally, vertically, or diagonally on the board. Make sure that children alternate being the first person to write.

3. FIRST LETTERS TO WRITE

First letters (A, H, i, I, l, M, o, O, t, T, v, V, w, W, x, X), can be written legibly backwards or forwards, but other alphabet letters become a different letter, or no letter at all, when rotated. Most alphabet letters look like different letters when they are upside down. But directionality is a confusing concept to new writers. Understanding the concepts *left* and *right* may not develop before children are six, so young writers often reverse their letters.

To create an easy writing exercise, print one of the *first letters* on every other line of a children's writing tablet. Demonstrate appropriate formation of each letter, then have children practice writing letters across each line. Act impressed with a child's first writing because starting to write is an impressive accomplishment!

4. FIRST WORDS TO WRITE

When you're teaching children to write, use *first words* that don't change meaning when their letters are reversed: I, HAT, Hi! Hill, ill, HAM, HOT, lit, OH! OHIO, OW! Ox, MA'AM, MAT, Moo! MOM, Mill, till, to, TOM, too, tot, tow, VAT, will, wow. To create writing exercises using these first words, fold lined paper so one word can head each column. New writers can copy these words several times under your model.

5. FIRST PHRASES TO WRITE

New writers will enjoy *first phrases* that use reversible alphabet letters.

WOW! HAM! MMM . . .
OW! HOT HAM, MA'AM!
TOO HOT, MOM!

Although alphabet letters C, D, E, L and S do require understanding of directionality, children enjoy reading and writing these *first sentences.*

I LOVE MOM. MOM LOVES ME.
I LOVE DAD. DAD LOVES ME.
I LOVE SIS. SIS LOVES ME.
I LOVE THE CAT IN THE HAT!

6. I LOVE TO EAT

Fold drawing paper into three vertical columns. Ask children to draw a food they love in each column, for example, *apples, bananas, cheese, chicken, frozen yogurt, hamburgers, hot dogs, ice cream, lasagna, macaroni, pickles, pizza, sandwiches . . .* When the children name these items, you can label their favorite foods. Then ask each child to dictate one sentence to be written across the bottom of the paper.

> *I love to eat fried chicken.*
> *My mom makes good spaghetti.*
> *I don't like peas and carrots.*
> *I hate squash and spinach.*
> *I drink grape juice or apple juice.*

7. A WISH LIST

Take dictation from the children for five sentences starting with the words *I wish*. To spark children's ideas, say, "Let's pretend we can wish for anything we want. What would your wishes be?"

Use additional prompts like *I wish that . . . I wish for . . . I wish you . . . I wish that . . . I wish I had . . . I wish I could.* If the sentences that children dictate make more sense in a different order, rearrange them to create a prose poem. Print or type the poem on the bottom of a sheet of drawing paper, to be illustrated by the child.

> *I wish I had a cat,*
> *I wish I could fly,*
> *I wish I were a witch,*
> *I wish I could do magic.*
>
> *I wish I had a horse,*
> *I wish I had my own room,*
> *I wish that beds could really fly,*
> *I wish it was my birthday.*

8. BUNCHES OF POETRY

A variation on the wishing poem is called *Better in Bunches*. Ask children to complete the following poem, replacing the underlined words with personal favorites.

> <u>Cookies</u> are better in bunches.
> <u>Flowers</u> are better in bunches.
> <u>Chips</u> in a bunch,

> I'll take in my lunch,
> And I might even eat them,
> Munch! Munch!

9. DIFFERENT ANIMALS

Fold pieces of drawing paper in half. Read a book about animals to your children, or show them some animal photos. Ask the children to draw two animals, one that they love, and one that they don't like very much. Label each animal, such as *ape, bear, bird, cat, cow, crab, dog, frog, horse, lion, lizard, monkey, skunk, tiger, zebra*. Write a dictated comment under each label.

> I have a dog that licks me.
> I'm afraid of big dogs.
> My sister has a bird in a cage.
> I saw snakes at the zoo.
> A deer ran into our car.

10. REFLECTIONS OF NAMES

Fold a piece of drawing paper vertically in half. With a ruler, draw a pen line on the middle six inches of the fold. Turning the paper sideways, have children print their first names in dark crayon on the line drawn across the middle of the paper and have children decorate their name with lighter crayons.

When no children are around, use a warm iron on the folded paper, melting the crayon wax to create a reflection of the child's name under the line. *Reflections of Names* make interesting bulletin boards that let children practice reading.

11. MINING INTERESTS

Ask children to imagine what story they most want to hear, what movie they most want to see, or what book they would want to read, even if no one has written this book yet. Your children's brainstorming can be displayed on a bulletin board titled, *These Are Our Present Interests* or *Our Interests for Now*.

12. CREATING FIRST BOOKS

Produce small books to be illustrated by the children themselves. Title and author are printed on a construction paper cover, and pages between the covers can be of newsprint or typing paper. Both the covers and pages can be cut into an interesting shape by grown-ups, then assembled and stapled along one side for the binding.

Small books can be made for many letters of the alphabet with covers cut in the shape of the letter, such as *O WORDS, T WORDS, L WORDS*. Children draw items beginning with that letter on each page, and a grown-up writes the word for them.

The pages in MY WHEEL BOOK are round. On the bottom of each page is printed, *A bus has wheels, A wagon has wheels, A bike has wheels,* or *A truck has wheels.*

SUNNY DAYS can be a round book or can be trimmed with points to simulate rays. On each page children dictate a completion to a sentence starter like *On a sunny day: I play ball, I jump rope, I draw on the sidewalk, I run home . . .*

RAINY DAYS is made of blue construction paper cut in the shape of a drop of water. The starter is *On a rainy day: I watch the rain, play in the rain, collect rain, play inside, have a friend over, look for rainbows, splash in puddles, wear boots.*

SPOOKY WORDS is made of black construction paper cut in the shape of a tall house with a chimney on top, to represent a haunted house. The starter phrase is *In a haunted house there is: a ghost, a black cat, a skeleton, a bat, a monster . . .*

ALL THE COLORS IN THE RAINBOW has the name of one color printed on the bottom of each page, with space for a child to copy the color word and draw a colorful item. Red can suggest an apple or a fire engine, but brown might suggest a bear or a tree trunk.

PRIMARY SCHOOL WRITING EXERCISES

1. WRITING A MENU

Many restaurants offer menus for customers to take home. Show the children a restaurant menu and suggest they create their own menus for an imaginary lunch. Take dictation from children to fill in the blanks below. These menus will be decorated by children and sent home to inform their families.

MY DREAM MEAL: A MENU

Appetizer: _____
Beverage: _____
Salad: _____
Main Course: _____
Side Dishes: _____
Dessert: _____

2. SHOPPING LIST

Children write a shopping list for an imaginary trip to a grocery store. You can use this list on a field trip, or send it home for families to use. The list can include *drinks, fruits, and vegetables; ingredients for a main course like meat, fish, tofu, rice, beans, and pasta; bread or rolls; and treats like ice cream or pie.* A master list of foods can be posted in the classroom so children can write their own shopping list, or an adult can take dictation from the children.

3. POETRY ABOUT FEELINGS

Create a FEELINGS chart listing eight emotions illustrated with simple line drawings like a smiley face: *angry, excited, friendly, happy, lonely, proud, sad, worried.* Have each child choose one feeling as the title of a poem. Collect the poems about feelings to be copied as a booklet for all the children in your class.

HAPPY by Laura, age 6

Tomorrow is a day closer
To my birthday!
When it is my birthday
I will be extremely happy!
My birthday is in June!

MAD by Jeff, age 6

Mad is stompy,
Mad is pouting.

HAPPY by Jeff, age 6

Happy is having a hamster,
Happy is having a good friend.
Happy is going to a friend's house,
Happy is having a good Mom.

4. DESCRIBING A DAY

Children describe one day in detail starting with this sentence: *Today was dull,* or *exciting, great, happy, hard, nice, sad, terrible, unusual, wonderful.* Children's descriptions are dictated to grown-ups. With a little spelling help, those children who already use manuscript can write their own descriptions.

A GREAT DAY by Julia, age 6

Today was a great day! Except for library. I had Tap. It was fun! Linnet is sick at home. Sometimes I wish I did not have my sister. My name is Julia. I have a friend named Krista. I play with her all the time. It is fun. We usually stay inside. We do things with beads. I do lots of things in my life. They're always fun!!!

5. COPYING QUOTES

Children copy a quotation written by a teacher and then illustrate this quote. Copying great writing by the masters offers good reading and writing practice, and illustrated quotes make nice presents and greeting cards. Find other poems in *Appendix IX, Quotations to Copy*. Longer quotes can be copied over several days. We don't want to bore children with what my teachers called *board work*!

AN ANONYMOUS NURSERY RHYME

Girls and boys come out to play
The moon it shines as bright as day.
Leave your supper and leave your sleep
Come with your playfellow into the street;
Come with a whoop and come with a call,
Come with goodwill, or come not at all . . .

BROOMS by Dorothy Aldis

On stormy days
When the wind is high
Tall trees are brooms
Sweeping the sky.
They swish their branches
In buckets of rain,
And swash and sweep it
Blue again.

THE SECRET SITS by Robert Frost

We dance round in a ring and suppose,
But the Secret sits in the middle and knows.

6. ALLITERATION IN POETRY

Explain to students that alliteration is the repetition of consonant sounds in prose or poetry. Repeated sounds contribute to the meaning of poems.

SILLY ALLITERATION by Julia, age 9 ½

I wish I was a purple puppy,
In a pig pen in Paris.
I wish I was a silver snake,
In a swimming pool in Singapore: sssssssss!

7. MY BOOK ABOUT ME

Use the following template to help children create their first autobiography. Discuss the difference between *autobiography* and *biography*, then help children find examples of both genres at the library, or read some short examples aloud.

Older children may be able to fill in the blanks themselves, but this book is actually designed for children who don't write yet. A parent or other teacher can fill in the blanks, taking dictation from the child. When the writing is finished, an adult should cut the page into strips to be pasted on the bottoms of sheets of plain white paper. The child can create an illustration above each caption. Note that a page number comes before each caption so you can easily organize the completed book, to be stapled or bound with yarn. Use the title page as the cover of the book.

MY BOOK ABOUT ME

By _____   Date _____

1. Here is my face. I am _____ years old. My birthday is _____.

2. Here is my family, _____.

3. Here are my friends, _____.

4. Here is my best pet, _____.

5. My favorite foods are_____.

6. A food that I hate is _____.

7. My favorite treat is _____.

8. Here I am having fun. I'm _____.

9. Here is my home. My address is _____.

10. Here I am standing in my favorite place _____.

11. Here is the title of a good book, _____.

12. Here I am in my favorite clothes. Don't I look great? _____

8. FANTASY VEHICLES

Read aloud a book that includes a fantasy vehicle, such as

> *The Little Engine That Could* by Watty Piper
> *The Polar Express* by Chris Van Allsburg
> *The Twenty-One Balloons* by William Pen du Bois

Ask your children to describe their own fantasy vehicle, using prompts that encourage composition. Take dictation so children won't be afraid to use long words they've heard like *transmission* or *fuel injection*. This writing exercise can introduce the classic triggers: *who, what, where, when, why,* and *how.*

SAMPLE WRITING PROMPTS

> What does your fantasy vehicle look like? How fast does it go?
> Where does your fantasy vehicle go? Why does it go there?
> Who drives your fantasy vehicle? Who are the passengers, if any?
> When is your fantasy vehicle driven? When is it in the garage?

9. NAME ACRONYMS

Ask children to print their first names vertically on lined paper, skipping two lines between the letters. Beginning with a letter in their names, children choose a word or phrase that describes them. Take dictation to record their acronyms. Children might feel inspired to create an acronym for their whole name: first, middle, and last!

MY NAME by Julia, age 9

> *Just about the most*
> *Utterly talented writer!*
> *Likely to be an author and*
> *Illustrator for her*
> *Awesome books!*

10. MY BED

Describe your bed: *blankets, colors, number of pillows, patterns on sheets, size of your bed, its softness and warmth.* How does your bed feel at night? How does it feel in the morning? Do you share a bed? What would you change about your bed?

11. DREAMSCAPES

Children use table blocks or found items like cartons and small boxes to create a *dreamscape*, which is a sculpture of a place that does not really exist. Tempura paints can be used to put finishing touches on the scrap sculptures. A child can photograph or draw the dreamscape before describing it. Children's written descriptions are displayed with their sculptures.

A DREAMSCAPE by Julia, age 9 ¾

In my dreamscape it is silent. Nothing stirs as I walk through the passages. There are beautiful sights to see. Nothing you see gives you troubles. Nothing is dull. There is nothing like a flower or a tree. Everything is strange and new. There is one single thing to fear. The endless hole. If you fall in, you keep falling and falling and falling. Everything but that is peaceful.

12. STICKER PICTURES

Provide a selection of stickers of various colors and sizes. Ask children to create pictures with the stickers on plain pieces of paper. As they design their sticker pictures, children should think about a story. Colored markers could be used to decorate the sticker pictures. Take dictation as children describe their pictures, to be hung on a bulletin board. Julia's picture was made of only six simple shapes, but she obviously thought about her composition in detail.

A STICKER PICTURE by Julia, age 9 ¾

It's a house in the grass and the living room has a rug and the house has a yellow door and the house has two blue windows. The house is a very nice house. Everyone has a jewelry box except for their Dad. And the house has four closets and four bathrooms and in the kids' room there is a rug. And they each and every one has a shell collection. All the girls have pretty dresses. The kids have socks and the socks have lace on them. And the house is very big and the house is very pretty. It has lots of decorations on it and the shoes have lace too. One more thing. Everyone has curtains in their room. And the two girls' curtains are very pretty.

MIDDLE SCHOOL WRITING EXERCISES

1. HAIKU

Introduce children to the formal verse known as Japanese Haiku. Haiku is designed to capture a single moment in time, using only three lines of 5, 7, and 5 syllables. Haiku does not require rhyme, but it does require children to observe very carefully to capture the description of a moment, as in the sample below.

HAIKU by Jean Wilson

> *Christmas tinsel*
> *Woven with pine needles—*
> *Robin's nest.*
> *Female robin*
> *On my window ledge*
> *Building her nest.*

2. IDEAL OUTFITS

Children design and draw an ideal outfit, describing the clothing from head to toe. Adults label their drawings and ask, "Where would you wear this outfit?"

3. CAREER FAIR

What careers seem attractive to your children now? What are the children's first and second choices for future employment? Children dictate and illustrate their personal preference for a career using pictures cut from magazines and their own drawings. Display these on a bulletin board under the label A CAREER FAIR.

4. CORRESPONDENCE

Children write letters to people they love, to invite them to a school program like an art show, or to send them holiday greetings. Demonstrate the conventions of letter writing, including the *date, salutation, body of the letter,* and *signature.*

5. CARTOON SUPERHERO

Children imagine a cartoon superhero and dictate a description of their superhero, including information about their special powers. How are their powers used? What villains do they battle? What problems do they solve? Children draw a picture of their new superhero to illustrate this essay.

6. THE PARTY OF YOUR DREAMS

Children create a menu and a guest list for the party of their dreams. Does their party theme suggest possibilities for food and activities? Is their theme Harry Potter? Spider man? Sports? Roller-skating? Popular music? Favorite movies? My daughter Linnet's birthday party once revolved around a *gymnastics* theme, with sweat bands, a trampoline, light hand weights, and an exercise video.

7. GREETING CARDS

Children design a greeting card for a relative or friend, imaginary or real, who is graduating, getting married, is sick, having a birthday, or moving. The children can use pictures and words to convey their messages. They should include an *'imprint'* on the back of each card, indicating the designer's name. All the cards are displayed on a CARD SHOP bulletin board and can be sold to friends in class to provide practice counting money and making change.

8. HOLIDAY STORIES

Children write stories with a holiday theme like Chanukah, Chinese New Year, Christmas, Fourth of July, Halloween, Kwanzaa, or New Year's Eve. Children will be more inventive if this holiday was recently celebrated!

9. CONCEPT POEMS

Children pick one concept word like *dog, cat, poem, girl, boy, truck, apple,* or *hamburger.* The sky's the limit here! Start the poem with one short sentence. For the body of the poem, begin several descriptive phrases with the concept word. Children end the poem with a sentence that contains their concept word.

THOUGHTS ON BLUE by Stacy

I got up this morning,
Looking for the sky
And the sky was blue.
My pillows were blue,
My shirt and pants were blue,
Steve's pants are blue.
The blue jays are bright blue.
My Aunt Josephine, she makes blueberry pie!
But I haven't never eaten any . . .

10. NEW YEAR'S RESOLUTIONS

Explain that people often try to make changes when the new year begins on January 1st. Children write a list of at least four resolutions, then order them from most to least important.

11. WISH LISTS

Ask children to write a *wish list* for any occasion. Limit the list to five items, and remind children that a wish list helps them think about themselves. Luckily, we don't receive everything we wish for! What if all wishes came true?

12. GIVING LISTS

Children imagine five gifts they would give to other people if they were powerful enough. List all gifts, then choose one the class can start to work on.

A GIVING LIST

If I could, I would make a sick person well.
If I could, I would do all the housework for my mother.
If I could, I would feed all hungry people.
If I could, I would give blankets to cold people.
If I could, I would make sure that all children had toys.

13. WRITING PROMPTS

Children pick one writing prompt as the topic of an essay.

1. Would you rather ride a unicorn or a horse? Why?
2. What kind of dance would you do right now? Why?
3. If people were flowers, what kind would you be? Why?
4. If people were birds, which one would you be? Why?

14. SILLY SPELLING WORDS

My daughter remembers a fascinating spelling bee her sixth-grade teacher organized. Children learned to spell silly words from *The Phantom Tollbooth* by Norton Juster, such as *mathemagician, Dictionopolis,* and *Digitopolis,* as well as the author's invented words from the poem *Jabberwocky* by Lewis Carroll, like *brillig, slithy, fumous,* or *mimsy.*

You can add a magical incantation like *Bibbidi-Bobbidi-Boo* from the 1950 Disney movie made of the classic Cinderella story. From the 1963 Disney movie musical about Mary Poppins, originally a book by P. L. Travers, comes that impressive word, *Supercalifragilisticexpialidocious.* From Mary Norton's *Bed-Knob and Broomstick,* published in 1943 and 1957, comes a type of magic called *intrasubstantiary locomotion. Zip-A-Dee-Doo-Dah* is a snappy tune from the 1946 Disney movie, *Song of the South.*

The name of a two-headed animal called the *pushmi-pullyu* is found in *The Story of Dr. Dolittle* by Hugh Lofting.

Help children invent their own magic spells or nonsense words. Create a list of invented expressions to help children practice spelling and handwriting.

15. AN EXERCISE IN PROS AND CONS

When children have a decision to make, ask them to list *pros and cons* for each contingency, then to compare these lists and make an informed decision. Children can list pros and cons for various chores in the classroom or at home, for different desserts, for different activities on field trips, or for different sports. By listing pros and cons, Julia was able to choose the summer program to attend. This exercise helped clarify her thinking, although it didn't result in one clearly better choice.

A LIST OF SUMMER CAMP PROS AND CONS by Julia, age 11

Marie's Class: Pros	Caroline's Class: Pros
Learn more technique	*Have more fun*
More enforced teaching	*A little easier*
More challenging	*More air conditioning*
Be with friends	*More organized*

Marie's Class: Cons	Caroline's Class: Cons
Too strict, maybe?	*Might not learn as much*
Too disorganized	*Might be a second transition*
Not knowing expectations	*No friends with me*
What's Caroline doing?	*Wouldn't see what Marie is doing*

16. COLOR POEMS

Writers choose a color, then choose several phrases that remind them of that color, to create three to ten verses of a descriptive poem. This requires abstract thinking!

PURPLE by Julia, age 12

Purple like a gentle mist
in the morning
in the mountains.
Purple like geese honking
above you
in autumn.
Purple like the feeling
on a cold morning
Purple like the feeling
of an old black and white photograph
on your hands.

HIGH SCHOOL AND BEYOND

1. REPORTS FOR SCHOOL

When writing a report, children choose their topic from among several, but let children study something entirely different if they have a topic that interests them. Remember that an interested student is learning something!

From ABIGAIL ADAMS: ONE OF THE FIRST WOMEN'S ACTIVISTS
by Julia at age 13

An avid letter writer, Abigail Adams offered much advice to her husband, second President John Adams, when he was away. And as he was often away then, through the mail was how he got most of his advice. 'No Ordinary Woman' is right. She was a role model for all the women of her time.

Abigail Smith married John Adams in 1764 after a three-year courtship. At the time he was a young lawyer living in Boston . . . Abigail Adams taught her kids to become the president, and she succeeded and had something to show for it. She is the only woman ever to be a wife and a mother to a president. Abigail Adams was an unusually bright person. Her ideas were avant-garde and her thoughts were brilliant. She knew that women needed a chance to shine and she knew that they would. Abigail Adams is a joy to learn about and a figure in history that everyone can learn from.

2. ACTION POEMS

Ask children to pick an action like *swinging, running, eating, dancing, drawing, painting,* or *swimming*. Describe the feeling of the activity in detail, using at least three senses. You can read *The Swing* by Robert Louis Stevenson as an example of a classic poem that describes the feeling of an action.

PICKING BLUEBERRIES by Julia at age 13

Picking blueberries
is a sunny stretch.
Muscles squeeze,
arms reach,
eyes squint,
and branches swing.
Each plump purple-blue bulge
sings on my tongue.

3. BOOK REVIEWS

Children read and review a current book. They could look for one on the best seller list, or visit a bookstore and check out the shelves. Hand out copies of newspaper book reviews that the young writers can imitate as they write their own review. Julia wrote this book review at age thirteen.

Tender at the Bone: Growing Up at the Table by Ruth Reichl
(Published in Dream/Girl, issue No. 8, May 2000, p. 20)

Ruth Reichl, author of this delicious book, is a restaurant critic for the New York Times. This gives away the secret of her book, <u>Tender at the Bone: Growing Up at the Table</u>. I have never found memoirs all that interesting until I read this one, and I have found the secret; you must read the memoirs of people with the same interests as you. I love food, both the cooking and eating process, and that was part of what lured me into buying this book. The other part was that my mom was offering to pay.

The author's use of recipes, intertwined with writing about her life, is intriguing and in some ways more fun than the average book—for a cook, at least. This isn't just a collection of her favorite recipes, though; she writes the recipes into the actual story so clearly that you can easily understand the connection . . .

4. VISIBLE CHANGES

Students find two or more of their school photos taken in different years. They write an essay describing them at the time of each photo.

What did they look like?
What were their strong and weak points in appearance?
What did they like to wear at that time?
What were their interests? Their likes and dislikes?
What changes were due to normal development?
What changes were due to their circumstances?

5. SILLY ANIMALS

Use similes to describe the silliest animal you can imagine. For example, the animal would have a head like a _____, and a crest, nose, snout, mouth, beak, feet, hooves, or limbs like a _____. How would the silliest animal travel? How would it fight, or never fight? What would it eat? Where would it sleep? How would the silly animal find a mate? How many young would it have? Would it lay eggs?

6. POETRY IS IN THE DETAILS

Write a poem about the physical details of a person or an animal. Details often hold unstated meanings.

I WOULD LIKE TO GET A GOOD LOOK AT YOUR HANDS
by Julia at age 15

I would like to get a good look at your hands
before you go.
I would like to search your veins for clues,
press on your fingernails
To watch them turn white
before the blood comes back—
I would like to crack your knuckles,
and put my nose in the palm of your hand

because I know it's never been there—
I would like to run my thumb over your fingertip,
until I have erased the ridges that make your fingerprint,
until I have rubbed away your skin, rubbed it raw . . .
I would like to get a good look at your hands
before you go, but I fear that you are already gone.

7. HOW I SPENT MY SUMMER VACATION

Instead of asking children to write an essay about their vacation, ask them to write a poem that describes just one moment from the past summer. Describe that moment in the present tense, as though they were right there, right now.

From OCRACOKE ISLAND 2000, by Julia at age 15
(Published in Urban Hiker, November 2002, p. 78)

My sister and I
are dogs splashing in the waves—
spitting the salt water out of our mouths,
swimming against the current,
struggling to body surf . . .
My sister's tan and smiling
in her chlorine-blue bikini . . .

8. TWENTY WRITING PROMPTS

Use *Writing Prompts* to encourage children to tackle new subjects. Many members of writing groups use prompts to trigger their ideas. Prime your pump with prompts!

1. Describe your ideal friend.
2. Talk about your favorite shoes: color, fit, or where they take you.
3. Look back at your life. What accomplishments are you most proud of?
4. Describe a religion you would join if it existed.
5. If you could live anywhere in the world, where would you go? Why?
6. Who is your hero? Why? How will you follow your hero's example?
7. If you could collect miniatures, what would you collect? Animals, dolls, cars . . .

8. If you were a star athlete, what sport would you play? Where and why?

9. If you could play a musical instrument well, what would it be? Why?

10. Describe something you wish hadn't happened.

11. What celebrity would you like to meet? Actor, singer, dancer, politician . . .

12. Tell about an incident when you spoke words that now you regret.

13. If you were rich, what would you buy for your parents, siblings, or friends?

14. What is the most pressing problem in the world today? Solve it!

15. Write about your best physical feature: hair, eyes, mouth, hands, waist, legs . . .

16. A portal opens to a spot on the space-time continuum. Visit the past or future.

17. You can create a new TV series. Who are the main characters? Situations?

18. Invent a piece of furniture. What is it for? What does it look like?

19. What cookbook would you like to see? Describe two delicious recipes.

20. Why would you drink a magic elixir to extend your life? Why not?

EMILY'S PATH

One writer's path,
Can lead her through the world,
Reporting on her travels, or the news.
Another writer's path
Can stop just beyond her door,
But her words may travel
Far beyond her shoes!

CHAPTER 9

One Writer's Path

Eᴀᴄʜ ᴡʀɪᴛᴇʀ ᴛʀᴀᴠᴇʟꜱ ᴀ ᴅɪꜰꜰᴇʀᴇɴᴛ developmental path, but developmental changes of most children tend to be similar. At first development is loosely tied to age. Even published writers started out as young children with only childish skills. If books provide enough examples of written language, sophistication and complexity increase as children mature.

Samples of one child's writing demonstrate this typical developmental path. Julia's writing over time, such as her stories, poems, school reports and publications, demonstrate common writing conventions. Notice, for example, her repetition of words and phrases, and her use of conventional formulas like *Once upon a time*.

Fragments of thought and imitations of other authors are normal as children's writing matures, but notice that even a very young writer already grapples with serious issues like love and death. With experience, a child may be *already a writer at six or sixteen*.

PRIMARY SCHOOL

JULIA REDFERN, age 6

One day Julia Redfern went out to play.
Oops! One of the chairs fell on her way!
Her mother called out to her,
"That Julia Redfern!"

DO YOU, age 7

Do you read?
Well I do.
Do you write?
So do I!
Do you draw?
I guess you do?
You do everything I do!

A BEE, age 8

Blossom, flower, lilac, rose
There's a bee between my toes.
Rose, lilac, flower, blossom,
There's a dead bee!
Why don't we toss'm?

ALIKE, age 8 ½

Dress alike,
Know alike,
See alike,
Go alike.
Go alike,
See alike,
Know alike,
Dress alike.

THE PRETTY PERFECT WORLD, age 9

I wish there was a world
where there was no pollution,
and there were special wishing machines
that were only one cent.
You could say what you wanted into it.

And then press the button,

And it would instantly appear.

And in school you would only take classes you like.

I'M STAYING! age 9 ¾

I'm staying! I'm staying!

I will not go!

I like it here where I am.

I shall not go anywhere.

I'm staying right here!

You can't make me leave!

I am my own boss,

And I will make my own decisions.

I'm terribly sorry,

If you wanted to move me.

'Tis not going to work this time.

I'm regretful, but it's true.

I can't change it.

And do you know what?

I'm staying! I'm staying!

MIDDLE SCHOOL

EXCERPT FROM A JOURNAL, age 10

Dear New Pen,

I think it is horrible that pens don't have lives as long as humans. Pens deserve a longer life than us. They know so much more. They wrote most of it. Everyone loves a pen, and everyone uses one, even in the simplest things. Like taking someone's name and phone number when they call your sister and you grab a quick pen and napkin to write it on.

Pens are important. What they know is everything they ever wrote. A teacher's pen knows what a child did wrong in a math problem. It knows how to do simple cursive. A writer's pen knows stories . . . A pen hanging around the house knows who called at 2:23 . . .

Pens make good friends, as you will later. I'm sure you'll be a different pen that knows my secrets. Just like my real pen, you'll be a journal writing pen. You are going to be proud of it. Pens make the best friends. I will be sad about my old pen, but my new pen is already a friend.

A FAIRLY PERFECT WORLD, age 10

All around, people are waking up,
All over the world, people have friends.
Friends who love,
Friends who care,
Who can change it.
Who can say,
"All over the world, people are friends."
That's how it will be,
We'll make world peace.
No countries fighting.
We'll all be happy,
No one sad.
No presidents,
No one to say, "No."

A DREAMER'S HAVEN, age 10

Lost in it.
The sky.
Fairy dreams.
Angels whisper together.
I read for moons to come.
Stars play and swim
In the light pool.

A BIRD, age 10

A bird's round head turns,
His sharp beak threatening,
Flies away quickly.
Daisies are swinging
To the beat of the soft breeze,
Swinging in deep thought.
A girl steps on grass.
It crumples under her weight,
Injured, but not dead.

THE DRAGON'S VISIT, age 10

Dragon, dragon,
In the night.
The whispers of your smoke
Awakened me tonight.
Smoke in awkward, curly shapes . . .
Your freedom shines brightly
Through your shiny turquoise scales . . .
You are elegant, and stand out.
Dragon, please tell me,
Tell me your stories.
You know them, I'm sure.
Of rainbows, of wind,
Of all animals invented . . .
Dragon, dragon, tell me please?
Who else has been your company?
Be it wind, or snow, I want to know!
Please tell me now, or if you won't,
I'll tell of mine, of my secrets, my company . . .
What lies beneath those big gold eyes?
What secrets do they hold?

LETTER TO THE EDITOR, age 11
(Published in *Stone Soup*, November-December 1998, p.3)

This letter is to thank you for your wonderful magazine. I received a copy of it in the mail from my aunt, and she said she recommended it. After reading it, I find myself recommending it to all my friends! It's a fabulous idea to celebrate writing by children . . .

MAIN ARTICLE, age 11
(Excerpts from *Goddess, A Magazine of the Arts for Girls* (Privately published)

Cicely Mary Barker and Her Flower Faeries

Cicely Mary Barker was a very talented artist. She painted flower faeries and made a whole series of books with her paintings. She also wrote poetry about the different faeries and the plants they represented. Her books sell now almost as much as they did in 1923, when her first book was published.

Cicely Mary Barker was born in Croyden, South London. She had to be taught at home because she had an illness, but she taught herself to paint and draw. Her parents encouraged this and one of the ways they did this was to enroll her in evening art classes at the Croyden Art Society. The first time she was recognized, not to mention published, was when she was fifteen and she had a collection of postcards accepted for publication. But it was Cicely's flower faeries that made her famous. In 1923 she published the first of the series, *Flower Faeries of the Spring*. She used the children at her sister's kindergarten as models, making her charming depictions of plants into beautiful portraits . . . .

BOOK REVIEW, age 11

Tomorrow's Sphinx by Clare Bell

In *Tomorrow's Sphinx* by Clare Bell, the world has been deserted by all humans. A wonderful part of this story is figuring out why, because the book never tells you. A young cheetah named Kichebo is left alone in the den, waiting for her mother to come home with her kill. Her mother has been captured by strange two-legged creatures while she was hunting, and Kichebo doesn't know this. Kichebo's aunts come to take care of her, but later in the book they have to leave. Nasseken, one of the aunts, leaves for a mating circle. The other aunt, Beeshon, completely abandons Kichebo, leaving her to fend for herself. Kichebo discovers that she can transport herself to ancient Egypt during the time of King Tutankhamen's reign. All in all, this was a very good book. I would suggest this book to anyone who likes cats, ancient Egypt, or just a good read.

CD REVIEW, age 11

Tori Amos, from the choirgirl hotel

Being a Tori Amos fan, as soon as this one came out, I ran to my nearest CD store and grabbed it. This CD is a little bit dark, and a little more alternative than her other one . . .

Tori has also gone sarcastic with phrases like "ice cream assassin" and "lollipop Gestapo." This is a great CD. Go right ahead and check it out, but be ready for some different Tori Amos than you've ever heard. Great cut: *Raspberry Swirl.*

BOOK REVIEW, age 12

The Poet's Companion by Kim Addonizio and Dorianne Laux

Ever read a "guide to the pleasures of writing poetry" as this book claims to be? Think you're too good for a guide? Or do you think that poetry writing is everyone's personal experience and that a guide to writing poetry is like a guide to living? *The Poet's Companion* . . . was written for adults, but a friend of mine bought this for me, and both of us found that it works just the same for teens as for adults . . . Under *The Poet's Craft* (my personal favorite topic) you could find *Stop Making Sense: Dreams and Experiments* . . .

The *Twenty-Minute Exercises* section has many different ways to get your brain working to get raw work for the poem you wish to write. In other words, inspiration. It also mentions that it is nearly impossible to write one draft of a poem in twenty minutes and have it be exactly as you like it. I beg to differ . . .

EXCERPT FROM FICTION, age 12

Finding the Dragon's Egg

"Um . . . I lost track of time?" Helena tried. Her parents didn't answer. They just stood, arms crossed. "But if I told you, you wouldn't believe me," she said. They really weren't going to buy this one.

"Honey, just tell us. We won't think you're crazy," her father said. Oh, but you would, Helena thought to herself.

"All right, but you have to promise not to send me to bed early saying l think you need some rest, honey, because even though I sound insane, it's true, I swear. O.K. Well, I was trying to catch the bus home when I tripped over something. That something was a dragon's egg."

Helena went on, "Right. It was this weird shade of yellowish-tan. It had little black speckles on it, too. So I tripped over this dragon egg and it cracked. I heard little wails from inside and I decided not to look. I just shoved it into my backpack. I knew I had to take it to the museum to be taken care of so I quickly grabbed the bus. But I asked the bus driver if he would take me to the museum instead of home. He said yes. But when I talked to the people at the museum, they rushed me by car to some fancy science lab. By then it was five o'clock, which I know was my curfew. I know I should have called but I was too excited."

She stopped to catch her breath. "How many times in your life are you going to discover a real live dragon's egg?" All this explaining was making her tired. And she had to say it fast enough so her parents wouldn't just put her to bed . . .

EXCERPT FROM FICTION, age 12

FAREWELL KATIE
(Excerpt from a story published in Stone Soup, September-October 1999, p. 8)

Anna Green lifted yet another heavy box from the stuffed back of her sister's silver Volvo. Not being very fond of physical activities, she felt sure that it was just this sort of work that was making her look "more mature" than her eleven years, as her sister had put it earlier that year, when the new doctor had thought she was fifteen.

Her sister, eighteen-year-old Katie, being older and more mature than Anna, had also mentioned that she couldn't understand why looking older was so terrible. Anna now glanced around the woodsy college campus, and, walking up the steps to the building that her sister was now calling home, wondered how Katie could ever be happy here . . .

EXCERPT FROM A MOVIE REVIEW, age 12

ANTZ

Rarely do everyday moviegoers get to see two rival movies in theatres at once. They are usually a few years apart, maybe a few months. But this year, Disney's *A Bug's Life* and Dream works' *Antz* meet in the middle . . .

Z, the main character, is a worker ant, the individualist of the group, and while everyone else is working away without suspicions, only Z knows that the ant government plans to wipe them all out, including the queen.

Not only the voices but the animation of this movie are amazing. Yeah, yeah, it's computer generated, nothing done by hand, but it's really quite incredible.

FORMAL VERSE, age 12

PHOENIX PANTOUM

> The phoenix
> A beautiful bird
> Flames and feathers
> Red and purple
> A beautiful bird
> Bathing in flames
> Red and purple
> Spices and sprigs
> Bathing in flames
> With heat and color
> Spices and sprigs
> Sweet rebirth

With heat and color
The phoenix burns
Sweet rebirth
Carry her to a new life
The phoenix burns
The glory and flames
Carry her to a new life
Like paint to canvas
The glory and flames
An immaculate throne
Like paints to canvas
The phoenix.

ESSAY, age 12

BEING SEVEN

I remember the day of my seventh birthday. I felt like the queen of the world as I blew out those candles. Seven seemed so much older than six, so much more mature. For the first few days of my seventh year, I walked around with my chin in the air. But when you first turn seven, though you may talk like you're seven, even look like you're seven, you're still six inside. You still feel like that little kid, that puny six-year-old. You still cry like a six-year-old, still think like a six-year-old, but you try to play it off like you think you can. With children of your own age or younger, you can.

I'd been looking at some candy. I picked up a bag of it and turned around to ask my parents if I could get it, when I realized they weren't there. My heart thumped loudly as my mind flipped back to six. Suddenly, the grocery store I'd known and gone to all my life grew, loomed above me, as my heartbeat became louder and louder and my eyes wider and wider. I walked up the aisles slowly, scanning them for my parents.

As I walked back and forth at the back of the grocery store, panic rapidly spread over my body and I shook and trembled with fear. It seemed they had disappeared, and my six-year-old mind figured that they had. Just then, though, my smart and mature seven-year-old mind remembered what my mother had told me to do if this happened, however. I don't think she thought that it ever would. It had just been a warning.

"When and if you ever get lost from us, go and find a grocery store official and tell them that you lost your parents." I was so proud of myself for remembering that I ran straight up to the cash register, a wide smile on my face, though my knees were still shaking a little. I found a free one, raced up to it out of breath, and told the cashier my dilemma. I realized suddenly that I was talking in a whiney young six-year-old voice and immediately changed my tone.

The cashier smiled a little and asked me what my last name was. "Sull," I told her, bewildered, wondering what she was going to do. Did they have some sort of record of the last names of each person who walked into the store?

"Could Mr. and Mrs. Sull please come to register nine? We have your child," I suddenly heard blaring over the loudspeaker. I was beginning to understand, but I was still too scared right then to think about it. Finally, I spotted my parents only a short distance away and ran in their direction like I'd never run before. It was over, finally over. All there was left to do was to put the situation behind me, never again wanting to remember.

HIGH SCHOOL

EXCERPT FROM A POEM, age 14
(Published in *Teen Voices*, Vol. 10, Issue 2)

SILLY POETRY

Is there a place in the world
for silly poetry?
Because people go deep,
and lose themselves in sadness and dark.
Maybe that's good.
Or maybe it's just not for me.
But if there is a place
for silly poetry,
please point me to it.
It's not that I'm scared
of the dark,
it's that the dark is scared of me.
And my poetry,

though I may want it dark,

turns on the light . . .

Perhaps I should dive in

and try something new.

But if there is a place

for silly poetry,

please point me to it.

EXCERPT FROM AN ESSAY, age 15
(Published in *Dream Girl*, January-February, 2002, p. 8)

THE ART OF THE MIX TAPE

Making a mix tape is the ideal way to share your music. Forget saving the world through hemp shoes and recycled toilet paper—try music! Making tapes for friends influences their mood, which affects how they treat others. Not only that, but mixes make the recipient pretty happy.

A mix tape is a tape with a bunch of different songs by different artists. Sometimes they have a theme, sometimes they're just random. Think of it like a collage: using other people's art to create your own art.

There is much more to making mixes than copying a CD. A mix tape is the perfect present: it's compact, personalized, and you can write funny stuff on the labels and decorate the cover. Everyone loves a mix. Even if they don't like to listen to it, the fact that you made it is enough to flatter them.

EXCERPT FROM AN ESSAY, age 15
(Published in *Cicada*, July-August 2003, p. 125)

EXPRESSIONS: DUST IN THE GROOVES

In 1983, three years before I was born, my family's house burned down. No one was injured, but the house was destroyed, and the memory no doubt flickered in everyone's minds for a long time after-ward. I've seen the pictures, the floorboards ending at obscene angles, the furniture indistinguishable from the walls and other various belongings. Knowing nothing about the fire except that it happened, I, of course, feel nothing except a detached sense of fear. Mostly, I just miss the record albums . . .

For now, though, I'm stuck on the White Album, listening to John Lennon sing my name over and over again, calling me "seashell eyes." I keep moving the needle back, listening to it endlessly, sitting in the corner of my room and watching the record spin slowly around and around, enjoying the crackling of dust in the grooves.

FIRST PLACE FOR POETRY, age 15
(Published in *Dream Girl*, January-February, 2002, p. 8)

PLAY

This morning
After a short night's sleep
And a droopy
Squinty
Wake up
I stood up
Salty and closed
And walked to my cd player.
I pressed play.
All at once
There was a twisty harmony
And a curly guitar riff
And there was music filling my room.
I could see it.
It seeped from the speakers
and stained my rug
before collecting around my ankles.
Now I could wade in it.
I could twist it around my finger
And smear it on my face.
It was cold
And fresh
Like exhaled breath on my legs.

It was blue.

I pressed play

And I was swimming.

EXCERPT FROM AN ARTICLE, age 15
(Published in the *News of Orange County*, March 20, 2002)

Nields played a key role in discovery of unknown bands

My friend and I were on our way to the Festival for the Eno, 1996. I must have been nine years old. I remember it so clearly, so vividly—the Festival was like a whole magical city unto itself. We were amazed by it. We sat down by a tree to watch a live band called the *Neilds*. Everyone in the crowd clapped and many sang along, and we did our best to pretend that we knew who they were, too.

In those not so long ago days, we still listened to pop music stations religiously. We didn't know about the wealth of bands in the world even in our own town, so we were intrigued by these new characters. There were two singers, both female, one with a guitar. We later found out that they were sisters, Nerissa and Katryna. The guitarist had blond hair like wheat and a steady voice, and smiled as she sang. The other was a brunette, dancing around, swinging miles of shiny hair all over the stage . . .

I find it hard to believe that I could have spotted such a wonderful band at nine years old "Almost ten!" whines my nine-year-old self. Maybe it was a glimpse of the me that was waiting in the future, beckoning through strums of Nerissa's acoustic guitar . . .

Influential Theorists of Development and Early Education

Bandura, Albert, 1977

Type of theory: social learning; role of modeling and imitation

Major concept: Children imitate the behaviors of people.

Bowlby, John, 1951

Type of theory: infant attachment; role of responsive care

Major concept: Infants thrive with healthy early relationships.

Bronfenbrenner, Urie, 1979

Type of theory: ecological contexts of development

Major concept: All aspects of their environment influence children.

Dewey, John, 1913

Type of theory: progressive education; interests affect learning

Major concept: Consider children's personal backgrounds.

Elkind, David, 1980

Type of theory: perceptual, cognitive, and social development

Major concept: Children's play is important for optimal development.

Erikson, Erik, 1950

Type of theory: psychosocial; crises of development

Major concept: Support healthy psychological outcomes.

Freud, Sigmund, 1915

Type of theory: psychoanalytic; the power of the unconscious

Major concept: Early experiences and traumas will affect later behaviors.

Froebel, Friedrich, 1850

Type of theory: organismic; kindergarten *gifts*

Major concept: Provide hands-on educational materials for children.

Gesell, Arnold, 1949

Type of theory: organismic; ages and stages described

Major concept: Children behave typically at different ages.

Gilligan Carol, 1982

Type of theory: moral development; gender roles

Major concept: Girls' morality centers on their responsibilities.

Hall, G. Stanley, 1891

Type of theory: descriptive child study

Major concept: Observe children's behaviors carefully.

Klahr, D. and Wallace, J, 1976

Type of theory: information processing

Major concept: The brain is similar to a computer.

Kohlberg, Lawrence, 1968

Type of theory: stages of moral development

Major concept: Response to moral problems related to age and/or stage.

Maslow, Abraham, 1968

Type of theory: humanistic, hierarchy of human needs

Major concept: Humans are motivated to fill their basic needs.

Montessori, Maria, 1907

Type of theory: self-correcting materials, child-sized furniture

Major concept: Learning environments, equipment must fit children.

Parten, Mildred, 1936

Type of theory: stages of play behavior

Major concept: Play follows stages of social sophistication.

Piaget, Jean, 1950

Type of theory: cognitive development related to age and/or stage

Major concept: Thinking skills follow age-related stages.

Pratt, Caroline, 1913

Type of theory: learning through play; standardized blocks

Major concept: Support play with time, space, and materials.

Skinner, B.F., 1938

Type of theory: mechanistic, operant conditioning

Major concept: Reinforcement promotes desired behaviors.

Smilansky, Sara, 1968

Type of theory: socio-dramatic play; stages of play behavior

Major concept: Promote verbal, symbolic, interactive play.

Vygotsky, Lev, c. 1920

Type of theory: socio-genic development; the role of culture

Major concept: Use scaffolding to support children's development.

APPENDIX II

Thirty Popular Circle-Time Songs

1. Alligator Pie
2. A Tisket, A Tasket
3. Bluebird, Bluebird, In and Out My Window
4. Did You Ever See a Lassie?
5. Doctor Catchall with Her Satchel
6. Down at the Station
7. Go In and Out the Windows
8. Head, Shoulders, Knees and Toes
9. The Hokey Pokey
10. If You're Happy and You Know It
11. I'm a Little Teapot
12. Jack Be Nimble
13. Jack in the Box
14. Jill in a Box
15. Johnny Works with One Hammer
16. Jumpety Jump
17. Little Red Caboose
18. London Bridge is Falling Down
19. Looby Loo
20. Mexican Hat Dance
21. Miss Mary Mack
22. Monkey See and Monkey Do
23. Peanut Butter, Jelly!
24. People on the Bus
25. Punchinello
26. Open, Shut Them
27. Ring Around the Rosie
28. This Train Is Bound for Glory
29. Way Down Yonder in the Paw Paw Patch
30. We're Going to Kentucky

1.   Alligator Pie

Alligator Pie, Alligator Pie,
If I don't get some, I think I'm gonna die.
Alligator Pie, Alligator Pie,
If I don't get some, I think I'm gonna die.

Take away the green grass,
Take away the sky,
But please don't take away my alligator pie!

2.   A Tisket, A Tasket

A Tisket, A Tasket, a green and yellow basket.
I wrote a letter to my love,
And on the way I lost it.

I lost it, I lost it,
I lost my little letter.
A little laddie (lassie) picked it up,
And put it in his (her) pocket.

3.   Bluebird, Bluebird

Bluebird, bluebird, in and out my window,
Bluebird, bluebird, in and out my window,
Bluebird, bluebird, in and out my window,
Oh, Bluebird, are you tired?

4.   Did You Ever See a Lassie (a laddie)?

Did you ever see a lassie, a lassie, a lassie?
Did you ever see a lassie, Go this way and that?
Go this way and that way, Go this way and that way,
Did you ever see a lassie, Go this way and that?

5.   Doctor Catchall with Her Satchel

Doctor Catchall with her satchel,
Through the rain the doctor goes.

Splishy, splashy, Squishy, squashy,
She makes music with her toes.

Doctor! Doctor! I'm so sick,
Give me a rhythm pill, right quick!

6.   Down at the Station

Down at the station, Early in the morning,
See the little puffer bellies, Standing in a row?
See the engine driver, Pull the little lever,
Puff, puff! Toot, toot! Off we go.

7.   Go In and Out the Windows

Go in and out the windows, Go in and out the windows,
Go in and out the windows, As we have done before.

Go stepping over doorsteps, Go stepping over doorsteps,
Go stepping over doorsteps, As we have done before.

Go forth and choose a partner, Go forth and choose a partner,
Go forth and choose a partner, As we have done before.

8.   Head, Shoulders, Knees and Toes

Head, shoulders, knees and toes,
Knees and toes!
Head, shoulders, knees and toes,
Knees and to-o-es.
And eyes and ears and a mouth and a nose,

Head and shoulders, knees and toes,
Knees and toes!

9.   The Hokey Pokey

You put your right hand* in,
You take your right hand out,
You put your right hand in,
And you shake it all about!
You do the Hokey Pokey,
And you turn yourself around,
That's what it's all about!

(* belly, bottom, elbow, head, left hand, left leg, etc.)

10.   If You're Happy and You Know It

If you're happy and you know it, Clap your hands*!
If you're happy and you know it, Clap your hands!
If you're happy and you know it, And you really wanna show it,
If you're happy and you know it, Clap your hands!

(* Flap your arms, Nod your head, Stamp your feet, etc.)

11.   I'm a Little Teapot

I'm a little teapot, short and stout.
Here is my handle, here is my spout.
When I get all steamed up, hear me shout,
Just TIP me over, and pour me out!

I'm a very special pot, it's true,
Let me show what I can do,

I can change my handle and my spout,
Just TIP me over, and pour me out!

12. Jack Be Nimble

Jack (Jen) be nimble, Jack be quick,
Jack jump over the candle stick*!

(*Children take tuns jumping over a block.)

13. Jack in the Box

Jack in the box, so quiet and still,
Won't you come out? Yes I will!

14. Jill in a Box

Jill is hiding, down in a box,
Will someone please open the lid? CLAP!

15. Johnny Works with One Hammer (*Pound fists on thighs*)

Johnny (Jenny) works with one hammer, one hammer, one hammer,
Johnny works with one hammer; Now (s)he works with two, etc.
Johnny works with five hammers, five hammers, five hammers,
Johnny works with five hammers, Now he takes a rest!

16. Jumpety-Jump

Sweet little Tony wants to jumpety-jump,
Jumpety jump, jumpety-jump!

Sweet little Tony wants to jumpety-jump,
Now sweet little Tony wants to bow down low.

17.   Little Red Caboose

Little red caboose,
Little red caboose,
Little red caboose behind the train.

Smoke stack on its back,
Going down the track,
Little red caboose behind the train.

18.   London Bridge is Falling Down

London Bridge is falling down, falling down, falling down,
London Bridge is falling down, My fair lady.
Catch a kid and lock her (him) up, lock her up, lock her up,
Catch a kid and lock her up, My fair lady.

19.   Looby Loo

Here we go looby loo,
Here we go looby lie,
Here we go looby loo,
All on a Saturday night.

I put my first hand* in,
I take my first hand out,
I give my hand a shake, shake, shake,
And turn myself about.
(*other hand, right hand, left hand, foot, etc.)

20.   The Mexican Hat Dance (Instrumental with dance)

21.   Miss Mary Mack

Miss Mary Mack, Mack, Mack,
All dressed in black, black, black.

With silver buttons, buttons, buttons,
All down her back, back, back.

She asked her mother, mother, mother,
For fifty cents, cents, cents.
To see the elephant, elephant, elephant,
Jump over the fence, fence, fence.

He jumped so high, high, high,
He reached the sky, sky, sky.
And he didn't come back, back, back,
Till the Fourth of July. Lie! Lie!

22.   Monkey See and Monkey Do

Monkey see and monkey do,
Monkey looks a lot like you!

23.   Peanut Butter, Jelly!

First you take some peanuts, and you crush 'em, and you crush 'em.
First you take some peanuts, and you crush 'em, and you crush 'em.
Peanut Butter . . . Jelly!
Peanut Butter . . . Jelly!

Then you take some bread, and you cut it, and you cut it.
Then you take some bread, and you cut it, and you cut it.
Peanut Butter . . . Jelly!
Peanut Butter . . . Jelly!

Then you take a knife, and you spread it, and you spread it.
Then you take a knife, and you spread it, and you spread it.
Peanut Butter . . . Jelly!
Peanut Butter . . . Jelly!

Then you take the milk, and you pour it, and you pour it.
Then you take the milk, and you pour it, and you pour it.
Peanut Butter . . . Jelly!
Peanut Butter . . . Jelly!

Then you take the sandwich,
and you eat it, and you eat it.
Then you take the sandwich,
and you eat it, and you eat it.
Mm, mm, mm, mm . . . Mmmm!
Mm, mm, mm, mm . . . Mmmm!

24.   The People on the Bus

The people on the bus go up and down,
       up and down, up and down.
The people on the bus go up and down,
       All through the town.

The wheels on a bus go round and round . . .
The money on the bus goes clink, clink, clink . . .
The driver on the bus says, Move on back . . .
The baby on the bus goes waa, waa, waa . . .
The mother on the bus goes sh, sh, sh . . .

25.   Punchinello

What can you do, Punchinello, funny fellow?
What can you do, Punchinello, funny you*?
I can do it too, Punchinello, funny fellow,
I can do it too, Punchinello, funny you!

(*Children take turns choosing an action the group imitates.)

26. Open, Shut Them

Open, shut them, Open, shut them,
Give a little clap! CLAP!
Open, shut them, Open, shut them,
Put them in your lap.

Sneak them, creep them, Creep them, sneak them,
Right up to your chin.
Open wide your little mouth,
But do not let them in!

27. Ring Around the Rosey

Ring Around the Rosey,
A pocket full of posies,
Ashes, Ashes,
We all fall down!

28. This Train is Bound for Glory

This train is bound for glory, this train*,
This train is bound for glory, this train.
This train is bound for glory,
Won't take none but the good and holy!
This train is bound for glory, this train.

*This train is speeding up now, this train . . .
Hang on tight as it flies by now, this train.

29. Way Down in the Paw-Paw Patch

Where oh where is sweet little Jenny*?
Where oh where is sweet little Jenny?
Where oh where is sweet little Jenny?
Way down yonder in the Paw-Paw patch!

Pickin' up Paw-Paws, Put 'em in her pocket,
Pickin' up Paw-Paws, Put 'em in her pocket,
Pickin' up Paw-Paws, Put 'em in her pocket,
Way down yonder in the Paw-Paw patch!

(*Substitute other children's names.)

30.   We're Going to Kentucky

We're going to Kentucky;
We're going to the fair,
To see a Senorita, (handsome hombre)
With flowers in her (his) hair.

Oh, shake it, shake it, shake it,
Shake it if you can,
Shake it like a milk shake,
And do it once again!

Oh, rhumba to the bottom,
And rhumba to the top,
And turn around and turn around,
Until you make a STOP!

APPENDIX III

Selected Children's Books to Read Aloud

Aruego, Jose and Ariane Dewey (1972) *A Crocodile's Tale*, (2001) *Splash!*

Asch, Frank (2011) *Happy Birthday Big Bad Wolf*

Bailey, Carolyn Sherwin (1931) *The Little Rabbit Who Wanted Red Wings*

Blume, Judy (1971) *Freckle Juice*, (1981) *One in the Middle is the Green Kangaroo*

Brett, Jan (2006) *Honey . . . Honey . . . Lion!: A Story from Africa*, (2004) *The Umbrella*

Brown, Margaret Wise (1942) *The Runaway Bunny*, (1947) *Goodnight Moon*

Burke, Tina (2007) *It's Christmas*, (2009) *Sophie's Big Bed*

Carle, Eric (1969) *The Very Hungry Caterpillar*, (1984) *The Very Busy Spider*

Degen, Bruce (1985) *Jamberry*, (1998) *The Little Witch and the Riddle* de Paola, Tomie (1973)
   Nana Upstairs and Nana Downstairs, (1975) *Strega Nona*

Donaldson, Julia (2004) *One Ted Falls Out of Bed*, (2009) *What the Ladybird Heard*

Dooley, Norah (1992) *Everybody Cooks Rice*, (1995) *Everybody Bakes Bread*

Feeney, Stephanie (1980) *A is for Aloha*, (1986) *Hawaii is a Rainbow*

Florian, Douglas (2003) *Bow Wow Meow Meow: It's Rhyming Cats and Dogs*

Francoise (1951) *Jeanne-Marie Counts Her Sheep*, (1953) *Noël for Jeanne-Marie*

Freeman, Don (1968) *Corduroy*, (1975) *A Pocket for Corduroy*

Gag, Wanda (1928) *Millions of Cats*, (1933) *The ABC Bunny*

Graham, Margaret Bloy (1967) *Be Nice to Spiders*, (1988) *Benjy and His Friend Fi*

Gwynne, Fred (1970) *The King Who Rained*, (1988) *A Little Pigeon Toad*

Heller, Ruth (1989) *A Cache of Jewels and Other Collective Nouns*

Hoban, Russell (1964) *Bread and Jam for Frances*

Hoberman, Mary Ann (1978) *A House Is a House for Me*, (2001) *Miss Mary Mack*

Imershein, Betsy (1989) *The Work People Do: Auto Mechanic*, (2000) *Trucks*

Keats, Ezra Jack (1962) *The Snowy Day*, (1967) *Peter's Chair*

Kraus, Robert (1970) *Whose Mouse Are You?* (1987) *Herman the Helper*

Krauss, Ruth (1945) *The Carrot Seed*, (2005) *The Happy Egg*

Lear, Edward (1994) *Nonsense Poems* (From collections starting in 1846)

Lionni, Leo (1967) *Frederick*, (1968) *Swimmy*, (1970) *Fish is Fish*

Lobel, Arnold (1982) *Ming Lo Moves the Mountain*, (1984) *The Rose in My Garden*

Mayer, Mercer (1968) *There's a Nightmare in My Closet*, (1983) *All By Myself*

McMillan, Bruce (1986) *Counting Wildflowers*, (1990) *Jelly Beans for Sale*

Mosel, Arlene (1968) *Tikki, Tikki Tembo*, (1972) *The Funny Little Woman*

Munsch, Robert N. (1999) *We Share Everything* (2011) *Moose*

Onyefulu, Ifeoma (1993) *A is for Africa*, (1995) *Emeka's Gift: African Counting Story*

Pallotta, Jerry (1988) *The Flower Alphabet Book*, (2006) *Construction Alphabet Book*

Peet, Bill (1965) *Kermit the Hermit*, (1980) *The Caboose Who Got Loose*

Pienkowski, Jan (1981) *dinner time*, (1989) *Oh My, a Fly!*

Piper, Watty (1930) *The Little Engine That Could*

Pomerantz, Charlotte (1974) *The Piggy in the Puddle*, (1995) *Outside Dog*

Potter, Beatrix (1902) *The Tale of Peter Rabbit*, (1903) *The Tale of Squirrel Nutkin*

Provensen, Alice and Martin (2001) *Our Animal Friends at Maple Hill Farm*

Rey, H. A. (1941) *Curious George*, (1952) *Curious George Rides a Bike*

Rey, Margret (1944) *Pretzel*, (1997) *Spotty*

Rice, Elizabeth (1969) *Benje, The Squirrel Who Lost His Tail*

Ricks, Charlotte Hall (1979) *Look at Me*

Rosendall, Betty (1972) *The Number 10 Duckling*

Scheer, Julian (1964) *Rain Makes Applesauce*, (2001) *By Light of the Captured Moon*

Sendak, Maurice (1963) *Where The Wild Things Are*, (2011) *Bumble-Ardy*

Seuss, Dr. (1957) *The Cat in the Hat*, (1960) *Green Eggs and Ham*

Slobodkina, Esphyr (1940) *Caps for Sale: A Tale of a Peddler, Some Monkeys and . . .*

Viorst, Judith (1971) *Tenth Good Thing About Barney*, (1997) *Absolutely, Positively . . .*

Wells, Rosemary (1973) *Noisy Nora*, (1999) *McDuff Moves In*

Williams, Vera B. (1982) *A Chair for My Mother*, (1997) *Lucky Song*

Wilson, Karma (2007) *Hello Calico*, (2011) *Bear's Loose Tooth*

Wood, Audrey (1982) *Quick as a Cricket*, (2000) *The Napping House*

Zion, Gene (1956) *Harry the Dirty Dog*, (1965) *Harry by the Sea*

Zolotow, Charlotte (1962) *Mr. Rabbit and the Lovely Present*, (1972) *William's Doll*

APPENDIX IV

Books for Older Children to Read

Anderson, Laurie Halse (2000) *Fever 1793*, (2002) *Catalyst*

Avi (1990) *True Confessions of Charlotte Doyle*, (1997) *Poppy*

Björk, Christina (1985) *Linnea in Monet's Garden*, (1999) *Vendela in Venice*

Boston, L. M. (1954) *Children of Green Knowe*, (1959) *River at Green Knowe*

Bristow, Gwen (1959) *Celia Garth*, (1971) *Calico Palace*

Burnett, Frances Hodgson (1905) *A Little Princess*, (1911) *The Secret Garden*,

Chevalier, Tracy (1999) *Girl with a Pearl Earring*, (2009) *Remarkable Creatures*

Crichton, Michael (1999) *Timeline*, (2004) *State of Fear* (2011) *Micro*

Creech, Sharon (1996) *Walk Two Moons*, (1997) *Chasing Redbird*

Dahl, Roald (1984) *Boy: Tales of Childhood*, (2002) *Skin and Other Stories*

Dessen, Sarah (1999) *Keeping the Moon*, (2000) *Dreamland*

Dodge, Mary Mapes (1865) *Hans Brinker or The Silver Skates*

Du Bois, W. P. (1947) *The Twenty-One Balloons*, (1950) *Peter Graves*

Enright, Elizabeth (1957) *Gone-Away Lake*, (1961) *Return to Gone-Away*

Estes, Eleanor (1944) *The Hundred Dresses*, (1951) *Ginger Pye*

Fitzhugh, Louise (1964) *Harriet the Spy*, (2002) *The Long Secret*

Fleischman, Sid (1990) *The Midnight Horse* (1993) *The Whipping Boy*

Fleming, Ian (1964) *Chitty Chitty Bang Bang: The Magical Car*

Frank, Anne (1963) *The Diary of a Young Girl*

Goldman, William (1975) *Marathon Man*, (1987) *The Princess Bride*

Heinlein, Robert (1958) *Have Spacesuit Will Travel*, (1981) *Tunnel in the Sky*

Herriot, James (1974) *Moses the Kitten*, (1989) *The Market Square Dog*

Hesse, Karen (1993) *Letters from Rifka*, (1997) *Out of the Dust*, (2003) *Witness*

Jackson, Helen Hunt (1881) *A Century of Dishonor*, (1884) *Ramona*

Juster, Norton (1961) *The Phantom Tollbooth*, (1982) *Otter Nonsense*

Lamb, Charles and Mary (1807) *Tales from Shakespeare*

Langton, Jane (1962) *The Diamond in the Window*, (2003) *The Deserter*

L'Engle, Madeleine (1963) *A Wrinkle in Time*, (1973) *A Wind in the Door*

Lenski, Lois (1941) *Indian Captive: The Story of Mary Jemison*

Lewis, C. S. (1950) *The Lion, the Witch and the Wardrobe*

Lindgren, Astrid (1950) *Pippi Longstocking*, (1981) *Ronia, The Robber's Daughter*

Llewellyn, Richard (1939) *How Green was My Valley*, (1954) *The Witch of Merthyn*

Magorian, Michelle (1981) *Good Night, Mr. Tom*, (1992) *Not a Swan*

Montgomery, L. M. (1982) *Ann of Green Gables*, (1984) *Anne of Avonlea*

Nesbit, E. (1899) *The Story of the Treasure Seekers*, (1906) *The Railway Children*

Norton, Mary (1943) *Bed-Knob and Broomstick*, (1952) *The Borrowers*

O'Dell, Scott (1972) *Island of the Blue Dolphins*, (1976) *Zia*

Pearce, Philippa (1958) *Tom's Midnight Garden*, (1978) *Battle o Bubble and Squeak*

Peet, Bill (1989) *An Autobiography*

Pope, Elizabeth Marie (1958) *The Sherwood Ring*, (1974) *The Perilous Gard*

Porter, Eleanor H. (1913) *Pollyanna*, (1927) *Pollyanna Grows Up*

Pyle, Howard (1955) *The Merry Adventures of Robin Hood*

Robertson, Bruce (1999) *Marguerite Makes a Book*

Rowling, J. K. (1997) *Harry Potter*, (2007) *Harry Potter and the Goblet of Fire*

Seredy, Kate (1935) *The Good Master*, (1940) *The Singing Tree*

Seuss, Dr. (1984) *The Butter Battle Book*, (1986) *You're Only Old Once!*

Siverstein, Shel (1974) *Where the Sidewalk Ends*, (2005) *Runny Babbit*

Smith, Dodie (1948) *I Capture the Castle*, (1956) *Hundred and One Dalmations*

Speare, Elizabeth George (1957) *Calico Captive* (1958) *Witch of Blackbird Pond*

Spyri, Johanna (1880) *Heidi* (1924) *Gritli's Children*

Suberman, Stella (1998) *The Jew Store*

Thane, Elswyth (1943) *Dawn's Early Light*, (1944) *Yankee Stranger*

Thurber, James (1939) *The Secret Life of Walter Mitty*, (1945) *The White Deer*

Travers, P. L. (1934) *Mary Poppins*, (1962) *Mary Poppins from A to Z*

Webster, Jean (1912) *Daddy-Long-Legs* (1915) *Dear Enemy*

White, E. B. (1952) *Charlotte's Web*, (1945) *Stuart Little*

APPENDIX V

Language Resources for Adults

Appelt K. (2004) *Poems from Homeroom*

Baker, A., ed. (1974) *Best Loved Nursery Rhymes and Songs*

Bragg, M. (2003) *The Adventure of English: The Biography of a Language*

Brazelton, T. B. & Greenspan, S. I. (2000) *The Irreducible Needs of Children: What Every Child Must Have to Grow, Learn, and Flourish*

Brigance, A. H. (2004) *Inventory of Early Development*

Bryson, B. (1990) *The Mother Tongue: English & How It Got That Way*

Childcraft (1949) *Poems of Early Childhood*

James, K. (2000) *Poems for Children*

McCarthy, D. (2000) *McCarthy Scales of Children's Abilities* (MSCA)

Miller, F., Vandome, A. & McBrewster, J. (2010) *Myers-Briggs Type Indicator*

Rogers, F. & Head, B. (1983) *Mister Rogers Talks with Parents*

Sage, A., Ed. (1998) *Treasury of Children's Poetry*

Schickedanz, J. A. (1999) *Much More Than ABC's: The Early Stages of Reading and Writing*

Trelease, J. (2006) *The Read-Aloud Handbook*

Tieger, P. D. & Barron-Tieger, B. *Do What You Are: Discover the Perfect Career for You Through the Secrets of Personality Type*

APPENDIX VI

Guides to Grammar and Editing for Writers

Amis, K. (1997) The King's English: A Guide to Modern Usage

Anson, C. M., & Schwegler, R. A. (2000) The Longman Handbook for Writers

Browne, R., & King, D. (1993) Self-editing for Fiction Writers

Cheney, T. A. R. (1983) Getting the Words Right: How to Rewrite, Edit & Revise

Hairston, M. C. (1998) Successful Writing

Lerner, B. (2000) The Forest for the Trees: An Editor's Advice to Writers

Strunk, W., & White, E. B. (1995) The Elements of Style

Tarhis, B. (1998) How to be Your Own Best Editor: Toolkit for Everyone Who Writes

Troyka, L., Gordon, E., & Dobie, A. (1990) Simon & Schuster Handbook for Writers

Zinsser, W. (1994) On Writing Well

A Dozen Quotations to Copy, for Younger Writers

1. Lewis Carroll, from *The Walrus and the Carpenter*

The sun was shining on the sea,
Shining with all his might;
He did his very best to make
The billows smooth and bright—
And this was odd, because it was
The middle of the night . . .

2. Elizabeth Enright, from *Return to Gone-Away*

Sometimes a story can open a world for you:
You step into it and forget the real one . . .

3. Kate Greenaway, *Little Wind*

Little wind, blow on the hill-top,
Little wind, blow down the plain;
Little wind, blow up the sunshine,
Little wind, blow off the rain.

4. Anne Hawkshaw, from *Little Raindrops*

Oh! where do you come from,
You little drops of rain,
Pitter patter, pitter patter,
Down the windowpane? . . .

Tell me little raindrops,
Is that the way you play,
Pitter patter, pitter patter,
All the rainy day? . . .

5.   Elizabeth Honey, *Back-to-School Blues*

Hair's been cut. It's neat again.
Got socks and shoes on my feet again.
Saddled with a bag as new as my shoes,
I got the mean ol' back-to-school blues.

6.   Edward Lear, *There was an Old Man . . .*

There was an Old Man with a beard,
Who said, "It is just as I feared!—
Two Owls and a Hen,
Four Larks and a Wren,
Have all built their nests in my beard!"

7.   Vachel Lindsay, *The Little Turtle*

There was a little turtle,
He lived in a box,
He swam in a puddle,
He climbed on the rocks.

He snapped at a mosquito,
He snapped at a flea,
He snapped at a minnow,
And he snapped at me.

He caught the mosquito,
He caught the flea,
He caught the minnow,
But he didn't catch me.

8.   Lilian Moore, *Ants Live Here*

Ants live here
by the curb stone, see?
They worry a lot
about giants like me.

9.   William Shakespeare, from *The Tempest*

We are such stuff
As dreams are made on, and our little life
Is rounded with a sleep.

10. Robert Louis Stevenson, *The Rain*

The rain is raining all around,
It falls on field and tree,
I rains on the umbrellas here,
And on the ships at sea.

11. Alfred, Lord Tennyson, from *Lullaby*

Sweet and low, sweet and low,
Wind of the western sea,
Low, low, breathe and blow,
Wind of the western sea . . .

12. William Wordsworth, from *The Kitten at Play*

See the kitten on the wall,
Sporting with the leaves that fall,
Withered leaves, one, two, and three
Falling from the eldertree . . .

A Dozen Quotations to Copy, for Older Writers

1. Maya Angelou, from *Women Work*

Shine on me, sunshine
Rain on me, rain
Fall softly, dewdrops
And cool my brow again.
Storm, blow me from here
With your fiercest wind
Let me float across the sky
'Til I can rest again . . .

2. William Blake, from *Auguries of Innocence*

To see a World in a Grain of Sand
And a Heaven in a Wild Flower,
Hold Infinity in the palm of your hand
And Eternity in an hour.

3. Emily Dickinson, *I'm Nobody! Who Are You?*

I'm nobody! Who are you?
Are you nobody, too?
Then there's a pair of us—don't tell!
They'd banish us, you know.
How dreary to be somebody!
How public, like a frog,
To tell your name the livelong day
To an admiring bog!

4. Langston Hughes, *City*

In the morning the city
Spreads its wings
Making a song
In stone that sings.

In the evening the city
Goes to bed
Hanging lights
About its head.

5. Anne Morrow Lindbergh, from *Height*

When I was young, I felt so small
And frightened, for the world was tall.
And even grasses seemed to me
A forest of immensity,
Until I learned that I would grow
A glance would leave them far below . . .

6. Ogden Nash, *The Canary*

The song of canaries
Never varies,
And when they're moulting
They're pretty revolting.

7. Steven Pinker, from *The Language Instinct*

In nature's talent show we are simply a species of primate with our own act, a knack for communicating information about who did what to whom by modulating the sounds we make when we exhale.

8. Christina Rossetti, Flint

An emerald is as green as grass,
A ruby red as blood;
A sapphire shines as blue as heaven;
A flint lies in the mud.

A diamond is a brilliant stone,
To catch the world's desire;
An opal holds a fiery spar;
But a flint holds fire.

9. Carl Sandburg, *Fog*

The fog comes
on little cat feet.

It sits looking
over harbour and city
on silent haunches
and then moves on.

10. William Shakespeare, from *As You Like It*

All the world's a stage,
And all the men and women merely players:
They have their exits and their entrances;
And one man in his time plays many parts . . .

11. P. L. Travers, from *Mary Poppins*

Bird and beast, and stone and star—
We are all one, all one . . .
Child and serpent, star and stone—all one.

12. Eudora Welty, from *One Writer's Beginnings*

In those days, the dark was dark. and all the dark out there was filled with the soft, near lights of lightning bugs. They were everywhere, flashing on the slow horizontal move, on the upswings, rising and subsiding in the soundless dark. Lightning bugs signaled and answered back without a stop, from down below all the way to the top of our sycamore tree . . .

Printed in the United States
By Bookmasters